WRITING FOR MEANING

A BASIC WORKTEXT

Michael Shea

Mercer County Community College

HBJ

Harcourt Brace Jovanovich, Publishers

San Diego   New York   Chicago   Austin   Washington, D.C.
London   Sydney   Tokyo   Toronto

For Maureen and Win

Where shall we find language innocent enough,
how shall we make the spotless purity of our intentions evident enough . . .?

Matthew Arnold
"The Function of Criticism at the Present Time"

PREFACE

Writing for Meaning: A Basic Worktext combines the usefulness of a brief composition text with the practical exercises of a workbook. Textual sections first discuss writing brief essays, paragraphs, and sentences, and then using mechanics to ease students into the finer details of grammar and usage. Exercises that can be completed, removed, and handed in follow each discussion section.

The exercises provide students with ample writing opportunities to engage them in writing and revising the language they use every day. These writing activities involve students in using their language more consciously and conscientiously. Interactive exercises require students to supply possible words, phrases, or sentences within a context. By filling in information in correctly written passages, students are encouraged to employ correct usage. Thus, no errors are modeled in the book, only language in various stages of development. An emphasis on revision throughout the book encourages students, sometimes with responses from other student readers, to go back over their writing and make it clearer and more meaningful. This eliminates the pressure of getting it right the first time.

In Chapter 1, "Writing and Revising a Rough Draft," students recollect their own past experiences to develop a topic. In Chapter 2, "Paragraph Logic," students support their ideas with the addition of details. In Chapter 3, "Sentence Logic," students combine words to act as meaningful subjects, verbs, adverbs, and adjectives. In Chapter 4, "Mechanics," students practice how the conventions of written language enhance meaning for themselves and for their readers.

Reading is integrated into the writing activities throughout the book. In Chapter 1 students read and question each other's brief essays before revising them. In Chapter 2 students read the first and last parts of an essay and then write their own paragraph to complete the meaning. In Chapter 3 students supply the missing words or phrases in sentences. In Chapter 4 students combine, reorder, or complete sentences to make them meaningful. In addition, in both Chapters 2 and 3, students are asked to read the openings of several short stories and rewrite them in preparation for writing their own compositions.

An Instructor's Manual accompanies the text and provides sample solutions to the text's writing exercises so that students can compare their responses to those in the manual. Also provided are (1) a "Getting Started" activity to orient students toward reading their own words more attentively, (2) suggestions for using the book's exercises, and (3) pre-tests and post-tests that make possible a holistic evaluation of students' writing skills.

I would like to thank my colleagues at Mercer County Community College for their support and encouragement, especially my colleagues in the academic skills department, and the reviewers of the text: Donald Cruickshank, University of Illinois, Urbana; Ruth Ray, Wayne State University; and Victor Villanueva, Northern Arizona University, Flagstaff. To Linda Decker and Gloria Reynolds my thanks for their hours of typing. To Margo Melchior my gratitude for her proofreading. Finally I wish to thank my wife, Maureen, for her advice and encouragement, and my daughter, Winnie, for her patience and good humor.

Michael Shea

CONTENTS

CHAPTER 1

WRITING AND REVISING
A ROUGH DRAFT

In the course of completing the assignments in this book, you will be developing your writing in two ways. Either you will be thinking about and practicing part of the writing process, or you will be rehearsing the process in its entirety.

In this opening section, you are provided with topics to write on, as well as directions for developing and revising what you've written. This continual writing out and revising of your ideas will allow you to improve your ability to use written English in thinking and explaining.

There are no foolproof rules for developing the skill of coming up with ideas, drawing out their implications, and then rereading and rewriting them in order to make them clearer. How explanations get written depends upon what has to be explained, who is doing the explaining, and who will do the reading. Even when the topic, writer, and audience have been identified, how these three elements of the writing process work together to produce a clear, believable explanation is still a mystery. Writers can, however, teach one another some tricks that will allow them, first, to free up their ideas on a topic and, second, to develop those ideas in more depth for their readers.

A most useful trick to use when you are trying to think and rethink in writing is this: Remind yourself that words have meanings (even a blank sheet of paper has, potentially, some kind of meaning). If you can get yourself to produce any words at all, they may bring to mind other words you might make use of while thinking through your topic. If you are writing on a fear that you've overcome, for example, you already have the words *fear* and *overcome* to "listen to" or think about. Play with these words in sentences until you feel the force of their possible meanings for you—the word *fear,* for example:

I fear heights.
My brother has a fear of water.
There's nothing to fear but fear itself.

Now you might try making these same points without using the word *fear*:

I am afraid of heights.
My brother is terrified of water.
There's nothing to be frightened of, except of being frightened.

At any point in this play of words and sentences, when other words and ideas come to mind, write them out. That's exactly the reason you're putting yourself in touch with the meanings of these words—so that they'll prompt you to recall related words and ideas, such as:

I am afraid of heights, and that's very inconvenient for me since I work for a roofing company. The first time I recall having this fear was when I was about twelve years old . . .

By this method of alternately writing and reading words that come to mind, you'll find that you'll produce more and more words and ideas having to do with your topic. If you have not been given a topic to write on, "word" one yourself so that you can begin "feeding" off the meanings of its words.

A similar technique for getting yourself started with writing is to set up a sentence that you might use when carrying on a conversation at a party, for example, about the topic at hand. You might even say it aloud to hear what ideas and remarks come to mind:

There is one fear I had for years, but then, a while back, something happened to force me to overcome it. I used to be deathly afraid of . . .

One of the proudest moments of my life was the time I finally conquered my fear of. . . . It was a fear I had lived with for what seemed like an eternity. . . .

You can make up these conversation-starters for your writing partner as well as for yourself. Also, you can ask one another questions about your topics in order to help one another generate a "starter" sentence:

Do you remember any special fear from when you were a child?
Did fears disappear, or become less frightening, when you became older?
Do you recall any fear that made your life very difficult at the time?

Then see what further ideas your starter sentence brings to mind. The trick is always the same. Listen to, or reread, your words attentively, letting their meanings bring other words and ideas to mind.

This process of conversing with and questioning yourself and your fellow student—much as you would at a party when talking with someone you like and respect—is also a technique for getting yourself to explain your idea or point of view in more detail. The "liking" and "respecting" is important. You're not looking for "errors" in one another's (or your own) talking and writing; you're looking to understand more about the meanings of the words and statements that together you and your partner are bringing to life through your reading and writing.

Questioning to find out more about what you or your partner have written is an effective technique when revising, as well as producing, a rough draft. Question words, phrases, and entire sentences that you do not understand or that you would like to understand in more detail. To discover what words, phrases, or sentences you'd like explained further, read carefully enough so that you can show the writer (especially when the writer is you) where you've gotten confused and explain how you think you got confused. For example, take this section of a writer's overcoming-a-fear composition:

> When my uncle ask me to join his job, I knew I had to face this situation of not climbing high off the ground. I just couldn't turn the job down so I planed a way to get over it. I visited our local playground twice a day, forcing myself to climb on the jungle gym.

This passage shows that the writer has gotten through the first—and often the most difficult—stage of writing. She's loosened up some ideas about a past fear. She has also begun to think about what motivated her to overcome the fear and how she went about doing so.

If you were listening to her explanation while having lunch with this writer, you might show your interest in her conversation by asking her questions about the points she's made. What questions would you have asked in order to keep the conversation, and her explanation, going?

If you were her writing partner, you could ask her the same kinds of questions. After reading her rough draft write your questions and comments in paragraph or list form, right beneath her rough draft. Ask questions about at least three words or phrases from your partner's rough draft. Ask questions which make as clear as possible how certain words, phrases, and sentences confused you or left you unsatisfied as you tried to put together their meanings. Write your questions out, below what your partner has written, making sure that each one refers to words, phrases and sentences that you would like explained further:

> What do you mean by the phrase "to join his job"? What makes you say that you "knew" you had to "face the situation"? How did you come to

know this? I don't think I understand how you're using the word "situation," and I find it hard understanding the words "of not climbing high off the ground": Could you say that another way to make the point clearer to me? Could you also make clearer to me what you mean by "planed a way to get over it"? Can you explain further how forcing yourself to climb a jungle gym helped you to overcome your fear of heights?

These are just some of the possible questions that would help the writer develop her explanation even more.

Avoid correcting grammar or punctuation errors (putting the "ed" on "ask" or correcting the spelling of "planed," for example), especially at the beginning of the revising process. The writer will often pick up this kind of error as she gets more involved in making her explanation clearer. Discuss only the words or phrases or sentences that have interested you, though they don't seem to tell you everything you'd like to know, or they don't tell you what you'd like to know as clearly as they could. What you have done for your partner—reading and questioning her rough draft attentively and respectfully—she will do for you, and, soon, each of you will be able to be both reader and re-writer of your own rough drafts.

The topics presented here are set up in such a way as to encourage you to write freely, to reread attentively, and finally to rewrite both freely and attentively. When in doubt about where to turn next in your writing and revising, always go back to the words you've already written. Let them speak more words to you, and enjoy the distinctly human activity of making meaning out of the language you and your partner share.

Exercise 1-1   Writing a Rough Draft

INSTRUCTIONS: Do each of the following steps as directed.

HOW I RELAX

STEP 1 • THINK

    Recall four ways you relax. List them below. Two samples are already listed for you:

        1. `listening to music`

        2. `exercising`

YOURS: 1. _____

        2. _____

        3. _____

        4. _____

STEP 2 • WRITE A TOPIC SENTENCE

    Sketch out a sentence to introduce your explanation of how you relax. Here are two examples:

        1. `When I'm tense, I use several techniques to help me relax.`

        2. `At the end of the day, I loosen up by doing a variety of things.`

YOURS: _____

_____

_____

STEP 3 • WRITE QUESTIONS

Think about each method of relaxation you've listed above. Imagine yourself performing each one. Then ask yourself questions about each method of relaxation—questions that a thoughtful and interested person who hasn't actually observed you relaxing might very well ask. For example, you might ask about listening to music:

1. When do you usually listen to music?
2. Where?
3. For how long?
4. What music do you listen to?
5. How do you play it?
6. What do you do while it's playing?
7. How does the music affect your mind and body?

Write out and number your questions on a sheet of paper.

STEP 4 • WRITE ANSWERS

On another sheet of paper write your rough draft by writing answers to your questions. As you write your answers, keep in mind that you want your reader to be able to feel he or she is performing and benefiting from the very techniques you're describing. Order your sentences in such a way that your reader will be able to follow each method, step by step.

STEP 5 • REVISE

Exchange rough drafts with your writing partner. Ask him or her to underline *at least* three words or phrases he or she would like to know more about in order to understand your methods of relaxation.

Ask him or her to write out the question he or she would like to ask about each word or phrase.

Rewrite your rough draft. The more questions you can anticipate and answer in your explanation, the clearer it will be.

Exercise 1-2 Writing a Rough Draft

INSTRUCTIONS: Do each of the following steps as directed.

A DIFFICULT DECISION

STEP 1 • THINK

Recall a decision that was difficult for you to make, since you expected that it would affect your day-to-day life. Here are two examples, but you should come up with a couple of your own:

> 1. deciding whether to go on to college fulltime or to work fulltime
>
> 2. deciding whether to live alone or with someone else

YOURS: 1. _____

_____

2. _____

_____

Make up three reasons for your considering each possibility and list them below. For example, for "going to college fulltime" you might write:

> 1. wanted to feel smarter
>
> 2. wanted a chance at a career

YOURS: 1. _____

2. _____

3. _____

For "working fulltime" you might write:

1. `wanted steady, fulltime pay`

2. `feared I wouldn't be a successful student`

YOURS: 1. _____

        2. _____

        3. _____

STEP 2 • WRITE A TOPIC SENTENCE

Sketch out a topic sentence to introduce your explanation of how you considered each possibility. Here are two examples:

1. `Just recently I had a very important` `decision to make. Should I _____,` `or should I _____?`

2. `I'll never forget the time I had to` `decide whether to _____ or to` `_____ .`

YOURS: _____

       _____

       _____

STEP 3 • WRITE QUESTIONS

Think about the reasons you've listed above. Recall what experiences produced each reason and imagine what questions a reader might ask you about each experience. For example, a reader might ask the following questions about "wanted to feel smarter":

1. Smarter than what?
2. What had happened to make you feel you weren't smart?
3. What did you think you would be able to do if you were as smart as you wanted to be?

Exercise 1-2   Writing a Rough Draft (continued)

4. What made you think that attending school fulltime would make
    you smart?

Write out and number your questions on a sheet of paper.

STEP 4 • WRITE ANSWERS

On another sheet of paper, write your rough draft by writing answers
to your questions. Arrange your sentences so that they explain each reason for considering each possibility. Your reader ought to feel torn between two possibilities, just as you did. You can accomplish this by
allowing your reader to consider the difficult questions you did when
making your difficult decision.

STEP 5 • REVISE

Exchange rough drafts with your writing partner. Ask him or her to
underline *at least* three words or phrases he or she would like to know
more about in order to understand your reasons for considering each
possibility.

Ask him or her to write out the questions he or she would like to ask
about each word or phrase.

As you rewrite your rough draft, take into account the questions your
writing partner and instructor have asked you about your reasons for
considering two modes of action. If answers to their questions will help
you explain your reasons for considering each possibility, make sure to
include them in your explanation.

_____

_____

_____

_____

_____

_____

Exercise 1-3   Writing a Rough Draft

INSTRUCTIONS: Do each of the following steps as directed.

MY PARTNER'S PERSONALITY

STEP 1 • THINK

Ask your writing partner what he or she considers to be three of his or her good habits and three of his or her bad habits. List them below. Here are two examples of each:

Good Habits:	1.	`concentrates well`
	2.	`uses time well`
Bad Habits:	1.	`gets defensive easily`
	2.	`is sloppy`

YOURS: Good Habits   1. _____

2. _____

3. _____

Bad Habits   1. _____

2. _____

3. _____

STEP 2 • WRITE A TOPIC SENTENCE

Write a sentence to introduce your explanation of at least two of your partner's good habits and two of his or her bad habits. For example:

1. `My partner's family and friends`
   `compliment her for some of her habits`
   `and criticize her for others.`

2. Just like you and me, my writing partner has both strengths and weaknesses, good habits and bad habits.

YOURS: _____

_____

_____

STEP 3 • WRITE QUESTIONS

Write out questions you'd like your partner to answer about each good habit and each bad habit you've listed in Step 2 so that you can come to understand what he or she means by each. For example, you might ask about having great powers of concentration:

1. When do you display these powers of concentration?
2. Under what circumstances?
3. Can you describe a specific example of being able to concentrate when most people would have trouble doing so?
4. What kinds of things distract most people from concentrating while doing something difficult but don't distract you?
5. What technique do you use to keep your attention focused on what you're doing in each case?

Write out and number your questions on a sheet of paper.

STEP 4 • WRITE ANSWERS

Ask your partner to write answers to each one of your questions. After reading them, if you have further questions about what your partner has written, ask him or her those questions orally and note down his or her answers on your question and answer sheet.

Write up your notes and answers so that a third person would come to understand each good habit and each bad habit. As far as possible, make your sentences recreate the details that allow your reader to visualize your partner acting out each of his or her habits.

STEP 5 • REVISE

Exchange rough drafts with a student other than your partner. Ask him or her to underline *at least* three words or phrases he or she would like to know more about in order to understand each good and bad habit.

Exercise 1-3   Writing a Rough Draft (continued)

Ask him or her to write out a question about each word or phrase.
Rewrite your rough draft. The more questions you can anticipate and answer in your explanation, the more your reader will understand.

_____

_____

_____

_____

_____

_____

_____

_____

_____

_____

_____

_____

_____

_____

_____

_____

Exercise 1-4 Writing a Rough Draft

INSTRUCTIONS: Do each of the following steps as directed.

ADJUSTING TO COLLEGE

STEP 1 • THINK

Most students find that being a college student is quite different from their past experiences as students. Think about the differences that you've experienced since becoming a college student. List four of them below. Two samples are provided:

1. not so many rules and regulations

2. teachers leave you on your own

YOURS: 1. _____

2. _____

3. _____

4. _____

STEP 2 • WRITE A TOPIC SENTENCE

Write a sentence that will make clear that you're going to explain how you feel and act differently as a college student from the way you felt and acted when you were a high school student. Here are two examples:

1. I expected that attending college would be quite different from attending high school, and I was right.

2. When I entered college, I found myself in a completely new school environment, so I had to become a completely new kind of student.

YOURS: _____

_____

_____

STEP 3 • WRITE QUESTIONS

Think about the new school experiences you've listed in Step 2. Imagine yourself experiencing them and, afterward, relating them to a friend. Write out and number questions that your friend might ask you so that he or she could experience along with you the new environment you encountered when you came to college. For example, your friend might ask the following about "not so many rules and regulations":

1. Under what circumstances do you recall first experiencing this?
2. Whom did you expect to give you rules and regulations?
3. What kind? About what?
4. What made you expect that such rules would be imposed upon you?
5. How did you react when such rules were not imposed on you?

STEP 4 • WRITE ANSWERS

As you write your rough draft on another sheet of paper, answer the questions of your imagined friend that help you explain each new adjustment you had to make. Discuss one adjustment at a time, recreating as best you can the confusion you felt and how you dealt with it.

STEP 5 • REVISE

Exchange rough drafts with your writing partner. Ask him or her to underline *at least* three words or phrases he or she would like to know more about in order to understand your confusion as a new college student and how you dealt with it.

Ask him or her to write out the question he or she would like to ask about each word or phrase.

Rewrite your rough draft, including in it points about the hows, whens, wheres, and whos your reader might need in order to feel as surprised and stimulated as you were when you went about the business of adjusting to college.

Exercise 1-5   Writing a Rough Draft

INSTRUCTIONS: Do each of the following steps as directed.

A VERY SPECIAL OCCASION

STEP 1 • THINK

Recall a very special occasion from your past. Think of five features or parts of the special occasion that made it memorable. List them below. Here, for example, are two memorable parts of someone's graduation day:

      1. `special breakfast`

      2. `graduation ceremonies`

YOURS: 1. _____

          2. _____

          3. _____

          4. _____

          5. _____

STEP 2 • WRITE A TOPIC SENTENCE

Write a sentence to introduce the memorable moments of the special occasion you're going to discuss. This sentence should remind you and your reader what you're supposed to be explaining in your composition. Here are two examples, but you should write your own:

      1. `I'll never forget how proud I felt the`
          `day I graduated from high school.`

      2. `The day I graduated from high school was`
          `the happiest day of my life.`

YOURS: _____

_____

_____

STEP 3 • WRITE

Explain each wonderful part of your special occasion in two or three sentences. Do this by answering questions that your reader might ask about each part. For example, he or she might ask about your "special breakfast":

1. When did you get up for breakfast?
2. Who was at the breakfast?
3. What was served?
4. How was it served?
5. Were there any special activities at breakfast to honor you on your graduation day?

Or, your reader might want to know about your "graduation ceremonies":

6. What time were the ceremonies and where?
7. Who attended?
8. What happened at the ceremonies that especially involved you and your guests?

STEP 4 • REVISE

Read your rough draft aloud to someone who is interested in helping you improve your writing. Add, subtract, and rewrite sentences in order to make your reader relive that special day along with you.

Exercise 1-6   Writing a Rough Draft

INSTRUCTIONS: Do each of the following steps as directed.

AN EMBARRASSING INCIDENT

STEP 1 • THINK

Recall an embarrassing incident from your past. Think of five aspects of the incident that made it embarrassing. List them below. Here are two embarrassing aspects of an embarrassing date as an example:

```
1.  picked up my date late

2.  wore the wrong clothes
```

YOURS: 1. _____

2. _____

3. _____

4. _____

5. _____

STEP 2 • WRITE A TOPIC SENTENCE

Write a sentence to introduce your discussion of an embarrassing incident. Here are two examples, but you should write your own:

```
1.  My first date was the most embarrassing
    moment of my life.

2.  I really embarrassed myself the time I
    went out with _____ .
```

YOURS: _____

_____

_____

STEP 3 • WRITE

Explain each embarrassing aspect of the incident in detail. Do this by answering questions that your reader might ask about each aspect. For example, a reader might ask about "picked up my date late":

1. What time were you supposed to leave on the date?
2. Where were you going?
3. With whom?
4. How late were you? Why?
5. How did your date act when you arrived late? Her parents?

Or your reader might want to know the following about "wore the wrong clothes":

6. Where were you supposed to go?
7. What were you wearing when you arrived at her house?
8. What was she wearing?
9. How did each of you react?
10. How did others react when you reached your destination?
11. What were the others wearing?

STEP 4 • REVISE

Read your rough draft aloud to a fellow student and your instructor. Make whatever changes you need to so that your reader or listener is able to feel the embarrassment you felt.

_____

_____

_____

_____

_____

_____

_____

Exercise 1-7 Writing a Rough Draft

INSTRUCTIONS: Do each of the following steps as directed.

A SPECIAL PERFORMANCE

STEP 1 • THINK

Everyone has attended a one-of-a-kind performance like a rock concert, a play, or an athletic event. Your assignment is to recall such an event and figure out what made it so special. Ask yourself the following questions— and whatever additional questions you think of—and write down answers that will later provide details for your rough draft:

1. What special event did you attend? When? Where?
2. With whom did you attend?
3. What caused you to plan to attend this event?
4. What had you known about these performers and their performances before you arranged to attend?
5. How had you come to be familiar with these performers and the quality of their performances?
6. What about the performance you attended was especially impressive?
7. How did the performance, or parts of it, impress you?
8. How were these impressive parts of the show superior to what would usually happen at this kind of performance?

STEP 2 • WRITE

Turn your answers into sentences as you write your rough draft. Anticipate questions like "By what means?" "Under what circumstances?" "Which kind?" and "What did it look, sound, feel, or smell like?"

If the following sentences help you think about your special event, feel free to use them:

```
I was familiar with many of _____'s
performances, but none was as special as the one I
saw last _____ .
```

To some extent, _____'s performance was similar to other performances of that sort, but, at the same time, _____ did things I had never seen done by anyone else.

For example, the way he or she or they _____ was extremely skillful, compared to what I've usually seen.

Also, _____ was inspired when he or she or they _____, instead of simply _____.

STEP 3 • REVISE

Ask a fellow student and your instructor to read your rough draft and question you about words they don't recognize or ideas whose details and implications have not been spelled out fully. Then revise your composition.

_____

_____

_____

_____

_____

_____

_____

_____

_____

_____

_____

Exercise 1-8   Writing a Rough Draft

INSTRUCTIONS: Do each of the following steps as directed.

BECOMING MORE OPEN-MINDED

STEP 1 • THINK

Picture in your mind your being in a certain place at a certain time, alone or with others. You suddenly say to yourself: "How could I have been so wrong? How could I have had this prejudice for so long? Why didn't I ever see how narrow-minded I had been before now? Why is the close-mindedness of my old view so obvious to me now? Why didn't I notice myself acting in such a thoughtless way in the past? How is it that I now realize that this old view misrepresented reality? Why do I now feel an appreciation of what I condemned before?"

On a sheet of paper, let your pencil think for you as you answer some of these questions. Cover the front and back of a sheet of paper.

STEP 2 • WRITE

Reread what you've written to discover what change of opinion or attitude or point of view you want to explain. In your explanation, be sure you make clear:

1. What your "old" or former opinion was.
2. How that opinion showed up in the way you acted.
3. What the circumstances were that influenced you to think again.
4. What about these circumstances caused you to think again.
5. What your new, more open-minded opinion is.
6. How this new open-mindedness shows up in your actions.

STEP 3 • REVISE

Hand your rough draft to a fellow student and your instructor so that they can write their questions about what you've written. Then revise your composition.

Exercise 1-9   Writing a Rough Draft

INSTRUCTIONS: Do each of the following steps as directed.

AN IMPRESSIVE PERSON

STEP 1 • THINK

   Think of a person who has impressed you. This person acted in a way that surprised you because you had never seen anybody act in that way under those circumstances before. He or she was a person whose way of acting, thinking, and relating to others stands out in your memory.

   Cover the back and front of a sheet of paper, talking to yourself about the kinds of things this person would do that would amaze most people.

STEP 2 • WRITE

   Write a rough draft relating the hows, whens, wheres, and whos of any of the impressive behavior you mentioned in your writing. Explain at least two examples of the person's impressive behavior. Include details of what he or she did that impressed you and under what circumstances. If the following sentences help you get started introducing and developing your examples, feel free to use them:

I first made the acquaintance of _____
when . . .

The first time I witnessed the way he or she _____,
I couldn't believe it. Nobody I had ever met had
acted that way under those circumstances.

And, as if that wasn't surprising enough, I'll
never forget how he or she impressed me the time
he or she. . . .

The way he or she acted then certainly showed that
here was a person who was not going to be
influenced by the way other people thought and
acted.

STEP 3 • REVISE

After reading your rough draft aloud let your instructor and fellow students ask some questions about the points you've made. Answer their questions when writing your revision.

_____

_____

_____

_____

_____

_____

_____

_____

_____

_____

_____

_____

_____

_____

_____

_____

_____

Exercise 1-10 Writing a Rough Draft

INSTRUCTIONS: Do each of the following steps as directed.

PROUD OF MYSELF

STEP 1 • THINK

Some of us think everything we do is perfect. Others of us think that everything we do is wrong. The truth, of course, is somewhere in between. From time to time, however, we do things that we ought to be proud of. These are usually accomplishments that have involved hard work, sacrifice, perhaps even pain. Because we worked hard and sacrificed pleasures to accomplish our goal, our accomplishment was all the greater.

Recall an accomplishment that you're particularly proud of. Ask yourself the following questions—and others that occur to you. Write down your answers so that you can think more about them when you write your rough draft. The more details you can recall, the more complete and developed your rough draft and eventual revision will be.

1. What did you do that you found difficult to do? When? Where? What made you want to pursue this goal?

2. What was so desirable about what you had to give up in order to pursue this goal? How did giving up certain habits, comforts, or pleasures help you pursue this goal?

3. What was involved in pursuing this goal that made you fear that, perhaps, you might not be able to accomplish it?

4. Describe the steps you had to take in order to accomplish this goal. What was so challenging or difficult or nerve-racking about each step?

STEP 2 • WRITE AND REVISE

Making use of the notes you've made, write a rough draft explaining how pursuing a difficult goal made you proud of yourself. Then allow your writing partner and instructor to read your rough draft and question the points you make so that you can write as complete and clear an explanation as possible when you revise your composition.

_____

_____

_____

_____

_____

_____

_____

_____

_____

_____

_____

_____

_____

_____

_____

_____

_____

_____

_____

CHAPTER 2

PARAGRAPH LOGIC

As you become more and more expert at revising your rough drafts, you will pay more and more attention to improving smaller and smaller portions of your explanations. As you reread and question the words in your rough draft, for example, you will notice that they tend to collect themselves into groups called paragraphs. A paragraph is a collection of statements that work together to explain a point—a point crucial to making clear your topic or point of view. This crucial point, usually best made in the paragraph's opening, is called the paragraph's *topic sentence*. In the following paragraph, for example, taken from a larger explanation of what the writer enjoyed about attending a rock concert, the writer explains how the audience he was a part of made the concert even more enjoyable:

> **The people surrounding me seemed every bit as entertaining as the performers on stage. One guy, sitting in front of me, wore a shirt covered with band-aids. He watched a rerun of <u>Leave It To Beaver</u> on a portable TV as he joined in singing whatever song was being performed and a couple that weren't. A girl sitting to my left offered me a baloney sandwich on rye and a bottle of grape soda if I wrote a poem in the notebook she had brought with her. The person directly to my right had dressed himself in an Elvis Presley outfit and sang "Ain't Nothin' But a Hound Dog." Occasionally he threw a scarf to anybody who would listen to him.**

Here the topic sentence is the first sentence while the rest of the paragraph's sentences work to recreate the experiences that provide the bases for the topic sentence.

Paragraphs, both their topic sentences and the sentences that recreate the experiences, will grow quite naturally from writing and revising your rough drafts. As you draw out, or question, the implications of your ideas—ideas like "people surrounding me" and "entertaining"—you will quite naturally write sentences that work together to explain them. You will be creating paragraphs.

Each paragraph ought to explain its own idea or topic in its own way, and the best way to achieve this is by asking the words in your rough draft to speak for themselves. In the example overcoming-a-fear composition in Part 1, for example, the statement "I visited a local playground twice a day, forcing myself to climb on the jungle gym" beg the reader or reviser to ask the following questions, among others:

Why did you choose to use a jungle gym to overcome your fear?

Can you describe, step-by-step, what you did on the jungle gym that helped you overcome your fear of heights?

Why "twice a day"?

Did you do exactly the same things for the same length of time during each practice session?

How did you act or feel so that you were "forcing" yourself?

Depending on how much rereading and revising of this sort that you do, you should find that your answers to these and similar questions will eventually order themselves into a paragraph. In this case the paragraph will recreate what the writer did on the jungle gym to help her overcome her fear of heights:

> **I recalled how I used to enjoy climbing the jungle gym in our local playground when I was younger. I figured I might practice there, gaining confidence one level at a time. Before I went to work in the morning, at about eight o'clock, I'd "work out" on the jungle gym. I'd force myself to climb to the next higher level where I forced myself to stay for at least ten minutes. Then I'd climb down. In the evening, after supper, I'd climb to the highest level I had gotten to that morning and make myself climb around the circumference of the jungle gym. Feeling a knot in my stomach and a lump in my throat, I'd carefully move my right hand and foot to the right as I practically dragged my left hand and foot to follow.**

As it happens, the kind of explaining demonstrated in this example is simply relating what the writer did and where, when, how, and in what order she did it so that she could overcome her fear of heights. She is telling, or narrating, the actions and reactions that took place as she grappled with her fear of heights.

Other points call for other kinds of explaining, as, for example, when you explain what you mean when you say "My room usually looks like a tornado hit it." The answers to your reader's questions about what your room would look like if a tornado hit it would take the form of a description of the sights of the tornado site you call your room:

My bedroom looked as if a tornado had struck. Blankets and sheets lay balled and knotted in the middle of my bed. Layers of dirty pants, shirts, and underwear buried my desk chair. Great wads of dust and lint had collected under the bed, while the braid throw rug trapped crumbs from cookies and pizza crusts to be trampled on and granulated further.

Sometimes, as you question the meanings of the words in your rough draft, you will find yourself sketching out answers that are causes or reasons why something happened or why something was like that. For example, the question "Why did you decide to return to school after having worked for ten years?" might be answered like this:

At work I noticed that those who got big promotions and big pay hikes were those who knew how to write and speak well, as well as handle numbers and computer languages.

Or sometimes you'll find yourself telling your reader about effects or results of something having happened or of something having been like that. A further question, "Since you've completed your degree in computer science, how has your work and life changed?" might be answered this way:

At work now, I not only make more money, I find my work to be far more interesting. Making use of my language and math skills, I investigate clients' communications problems and work out possible solutions.

For the most part, though, when you answer questions you've raised in your rough draft, you will discover that reasons or results and causes or effects will often have to be explained further by telling what happened or by describing something. In fact, a very useful kind of paragraph that will grow out of questioning the words in your rough draft is the paragraph that draws examples from your own experience by describing what you saw, heard, smelled, tasted, or touched:

Chet's dinner at La Mangeria was not worth the fifteen dollars he had paid for it. The plateful of gummy spaghetti was covered with a watery, greasy tomato sauce. The two puny meatballs were pink and mushy inside. The wine he was served smelled and tasted like vinegar.

Regardless of the kind of paragraph logic that grows out of questioning your rough draft, in your revision each sentence should do its share to help explain the meaning of the sentences that have gone before it. As you focus more on your sentences as parts of paragraphs, notice in what way each sentence helps you understand something new and relevant about what you learned from the previous sentences. Each sentence builds on the other sentences that precede or go before it. This working relationship between sentences in a paragraph is often referred to as *coherence*.

If you're confused when you read a paragraph, ask yourself or the writer how the confusing word or phrase follows from the points made in the previous sentences. If Chet's dinner were described in the following way, for example, the writer would need to be asked a few questions about how certain of these sentences are related one to another:

> (1) Chet's dinner at La Mangeria was not worth the fifteen dollars he had paid for it. (2) The plateful of gummy spaghetti was covered with a watery, greasy tomato sauce. (3) The dinner was certainly a waste of Chet's hard-earned money. (4) The two puny meatballs were pink and mushy inside. (5) La Mangeria advertised that it used home-made pasta. (6) The wine he was served smelled and tasted like vinegar. (7) The meatballs also tasted of too much garlic.

Here are some of the questions a careful and interested reader of this rough draft might ask its writer:

1. How does sentence 3 help explain further about Chet's having wasted his money on a bad meal?

2. How does the fact about La Mangeria's advertisement in sentence 5 help explain further about Chet's having wasted money on a bad meal?

3. How do the distasteful meatballs mentioned in sentence 7 differ from the distasteful ones mentioned in sentence 4?

In general, then, the work a given sentence does for a paragraph will be a matter of explaining a cause, an effect, results, or the sights, sounds, tastes, and other sensations that exemplify the topic. Your paragraph's logic or coherence will result from providing your reader with the imaginable details he or she needs in order to understand what you're explaining. How extensively you need to describe or relate what you have observed or experienced depends upon how clear your points are to your reader.

Therefore, the feature to develop in your writing is this recreation of the actions and experiences that have caused you to state a given point— especially a point that is complex or crucial to your larger point of view. In fact, much of your education in the humanities, the natural sciences, the social sciences, and applied sciences will take the form of your being asked to recreate what you have observed from reading a text or taking part in a "hands-on" experiment and, then, tell how those observations led you to certain conclusions.

The exercises in this section will allow you to practice figuring out from a rough draft what you ought to say next and how you ought to say it in order to explain where your ideas have come from. You will be asked to pay careful attention to the language of causes, effects, and examples so that you can develop such language further. In this way you will practice letting the words of your own rough drafts "read out" their implied causes, effects, and examples, even as you ask and answer questions about their meanings.

WRITING A PARAGRAPH FROM CONTEXT

The point of the following exercises is to show you how paragraphs are the building blocks of longer pieces of writing and how the ideas that support a topic can be allowed to generate still more informative ideas and facts. These exercises will help free you to think up supporting ideas for paragraphs and then to develop them in more detail. Most sentences in paragraphs will perform one of four purposes

1. give reasons for your saying that a certain statement is true.
2. give results of a statement's being true.
3. state examples.
4. recreate the sights, sounds, or other observations that explain your reasons, results, and examples.

The exercises will also provide you with the opportunity of rereading and revising paragraphs in the context of other paragraphs.

In the following pieces, writers have thought through their topics enough so that they present three main points to explain their larger point of view. However, only two of those points are pursued to some depth while one is left unquestioned and hence unexplained. Your job is to note how the writers generate details for two of their main points and then to think up details to make the undeveloped point clear and understandable. Here's an example:

A SUDDEN CHANGE

Every once in a while, your life suddenly changes in ways you hadn't expected. That's what happened to me the time my family and I had to move from Indiana to New York City where my father had gotten a new job.

The worst change I had to put up with was that I no longer lived near Wade whom I had been dating during my sophomore and junior years of high school. We were used to doing everything together. On week nights, after dinner, we would study together at his house or at mine. I helped him with his math, and he helped me with my English. On weekends, when we got out of work, we'd party with friends or go to a movie and then to our favorite pizza place. After I moved, both weeknights and weekends were lonely and dreary. Since Wade wasn't around, I was no longer interested in doing my English homework, and I couldn't even figure out how to do my math. On Saturday and Sunday, I spent my time staring at the television as I tried to pass the time till school started on Monday morning.

And speaking of school, I found it nearly impossible to get to know anybody at my new school. _____

_____

_____

_____

_____

_____

_____

_____

Another disturbing change was living in the big city instead of the country. In Indiana I had lived on a small farm near a small town called Boonton. Only a few thousand people lived there, and I grew to know many of them. I had plenty of space for myself, both inside and outside our house and trees, fields, and birds to enjoy everywhere. I could be by myself, very close to nature, or I could be with friends I knew very well. New York was a whole other way of life. My family and I lived in a high-rise apartment building in an apartment of only a few rooms. We lived on a street crowded with even more high-rise apartment buildings. I couldn't get away from noise either inside or outside my apartment. There were lots of people, no friends or neighbors, and no space for me to spend time with myself. If I wanted to see trees or grass, I had to walk a mile to Central Park which can be as crowded and dangerous as it is beautiful.

Until I began to appreciate my new way of life, letting go of the old one was a very painful experience.

Generate supporting details for the unexplained point by asking your-self what kinds of details would help explain the point. If you were making this point to a friend, what questions might he or she ask you about it in order to understand it better? What kinds of details might he or she expect you to introduce and elaborate on?

You might ask the following questions about finding it difficult to get to know anyone at school:

Had you been able to make friends in Indiana? How?

What about your new high school made it difficult for you to make friends?

Did you try? How?

Why didn't your efforts produce results?

If you imagine and answer such questions, you will be well on your way to explaining this undeveloped point as thoroughly as the other two have been explained.

After sketching out answers to these questions, write a rough draft of your explanation on a scrap sheet of paper. Read your new paragraph aloud to hear if it is as detailed and logical as the others. Reword whatever sounds confusing or vague, add answers to unanswered questions you should have answered, and then write your completed paragraph in the space provided.

Here is an example of what you might have wrtten about the difficulty of getting along at your new high school:

> **And speaking of school, I found it nearly impossible to get to know anybody at my new school. In the school I had attended in Indiana, there were only about four hundred students in the whole school. We all knew one another fairly well, and lived in a radius of a few miles. We not only went to school together, we shopped together, went to the movies together, and attended basketball and football games together. I grew up with the same kids from elementary to high school. At my new high school, where there were more than four hundred people just in my senior class, I wasn't able to get to know anybody. Everybody rushed from one class to another, and then they joined their friends. There were so many people in the school, I seldom even saw the same face twice in the same day. I joined the field hockey team and the glee club, but even under these circum-stances people tended to mind their own business or stay with their own friends. I felt crowded and alone all at the same time.**

Now see if you can do better.

Exercise 2-1   Writing a Paragraph in Context

INSTRUCTIONS: Supply the missing paragraph for the following composition. Write a rough draft and revise it before writing your paragraph in the space provided.

MY STUDENTSHIP

My first semester at college was not a very successful one for me. I failed my math and composition courses, while barely passing my psychology and criminal justice courses. In my second semester, however, I took all these courses over again and achieved a B-minus average. During the second semester I made some very important changes in the way I behaved as a student.

First, I not only attended classes regularly, I prepared for each class and paid close attention to what the instructors expected me to do, both in classes and outside of classes. When my psychology professor announced that he would discuss a certain topic from our textbook, I would read the chapter, underlining its main points and jotting down questions about words, phrases, and statements whose meanings I didn't understand. In class I took notes in my own words, asking questions when I didn't understand what point the instructor was making.

I also set up a daily schedule of activities so that my study time was not taken over by work or play.

_____

_____

_____

_____

_____

_____

_____

_____

_____

_____

_____

_____

_____

_____

_____

_____

_____

_____

_____

_____

_____

Instead of always being with the "students" who partied or cut classes to play pool in the game room, I introduced myself to those students who were interested in developing their minds and accomplishing goals. These were usually students who had experience trying to raise families, maintain marriages, and find satisfying and well-paying work. They taught me a lot about motivation, discipline, and the subjects we were studying together.

Since I've made these changes in the way I study, I not only like school better, I like myself better.

Exercise 2-2   Writing a Paragraph in Context

INSTRUCTIONS: Supply the missing paragraph for the following composition. Write a rough draft and revise it before writing your paragraph in the space provided.

AN UNWELCOME FAMILY MEMBER

I've finally concluded that I've got to get rid of my cat Geoffrey. Geoffrey has managed to upset everyone in my family.

My mother is angry about what he's done to the furniture in the living room. Every night while we're all asleep, Geoffrey sneaks his way from my room to the living room where he sharpens his claws on the legs of a couple of wooden chairs. He has taken the finish off the bottom five inches of all the chair legs. He also scratches the material covering the arms of the upholstered furniture; the arm rests of the sofa and chairs are in shreds.

My brother Mike is allergic to Geoffrey. Every evening as Mike watches TV in the family room, Geoffrey jumps in his lap and licks Mike's moustache. Mike sneezes, coughs, and gasps for breath until finally he has to hide in his bedroom. It has now reached the point where Geoffrey has left his hair throughout the entire house, so Mike sneezes, coughs, and gasps the moment he walks in the front door.

My father has the most serious complaint against Geoffrey.

_____

_____

_____

_____

_____

_____

_____

_____

_____

_____

_____

_____

_____

_____

_____

_____

_____

_____

_____

_____

_____

_____

_____

_____

_____

_____

    All these complaints against Geoffrey make it clear that either he moves out, or the both of us will find ourselves out on the street.

Exercise 2-3   Writing a Paragraph in Context

INSTRUCTIONS: Supply the missing paragraph for the following composition. Write a rough draft and revise it before writing your paragraph in the space provided.

A DIFFICULT JOB

Working at the local supermarket was the worst job I ever had. The work was hard, the people difficult, and the pay paltry.

I thought that all I would have to do was to charge customers for the groceries they bought. Boy was I wrong! For one thing my boss ordered me to clean the meat cooler every day. The cooler was the size of a fairly big closet and smelled of blood. Blood was encrusted on the sides of the cooler and stagnated in greasy pools on the floor of the cooler. Every evening from seven till nine, I held my nose with one hand while scrubbing with the other. Unloading the produce trucks wasn't any picnic either! For an hour a day, I carried fifty-pound bags and crates of potatoes, onions, and celery from the truck parked at the front of the store to the storeroom in the back, a distance of about fifty feet.

Not only were many customers difficult to get along with, so were my fellow workers.

_____

_____

_____

_____

_____

_____

_____

_____

_____

_____

_____

_____

_____

_____

_____

_____

_____

_____

_____

_____

_____

_____

_____

_____

The boss was cheap. He refused to pay above minimum wage so that forty hours of hard work brought me a take-home pay of about ninety-five dollars. He never gave any bonuses and charged me for every soda I drank while recovering from his slave-driving. Often he kept me working without pay after my eight hours were up.

Finally I quit; any job I find has got to be better than that one.

Exercise 2-4   Writing a Paragraph in Context

INSTRUCTIONS: Supply the missing paragraph for the following composition. Write a rough draft and revise it before writing your paragraph in the space provided.

AN EMBARRASSING EVENING

Last Saturday night my friend Larry invited my girlfriend Beth and me to have dinner with him, his girlfriend Ruth, and his parents at their home. I was happy to accept and looked forward to it. I had always admired Larry's parents. They seemed to be happily married, but that night I got a whole new view of them and their relationship.

After Larry's mother served us drinks, she asked me a few questions about my plans after I graduated from college. While Mrs. Smith asked me where I had applied for jobs, Mr. Smith interrupted her, demanding that she get some ice from the kitchen. We all smiled lamely as Mrs. Smith did what she was told. After she returned to the living room, we hoped all would be peaceful again. However, we were wrong.

Mr. Smith sipped some of his scotch, jumped up from his chair, grabbed the bottle in order to read the label. Glaring at Mrs. Smith, he shouted that she shouldn't balance her household budget by buying cheap scotch. Her face turning red, she got up from her seat and went into the kitchen to check the roast.

At the dinner table, I observed that Mrs. Smith was also capable of treating her husband badly.

_____

_____

_____

_____

_____

_____

_____

_____

_____

_____

_____

_____

_____

_____

_____

_____

_____

_____

_____

_____

_____

_____

I then recalled that usually when I met Mr. and Mrs. Smith many other people were present: at our high school graduation, for example, or at Larry's older sister's wedding. It was only when I was "alone" with them that I discovered what their relationship was really like. I was very surprised.

Exercise 2-5 Writing a Paragraph in Context

INSTRUCTIONS: Supply the missing paragraph for the following composition. Write a rough draft and revise it before writing your paragraph in the space provided.

ANXIETIES OF A GRADUATING SENIOR

In January of my senior year, it struck me that I would soon be graduating from high school. This important change in my life worried me. I had some important questions to ask myself, and to answer.

Should I, for example, continue to live at home with my parents and three brothers and sisters? To continue to live with them would be good in some ways, bad in others.

_____

_____

_____

_____

_____

_____

_____

_____

_____

_____

_____

_____

_____

_____

_____

_____

_____

_____

_____

_____

_____

_____

_____

_____

Should I continue my education? I hadn't been a very conscientious student in high school. I took the easiest courses I could and did as little studying and paying attention in class as possible. Therefore, not only were my marks low, but also I didn't have the discipline or the technique of studying. How could I possibly be accepted—or survive—at a college? And, of course, I had no money to finance any schooling. On the other hand, I knew I needed to be better disciplined, think better, and know more if I wanted to get a job that would be both well-paying and challenging. I also wanted to get to know people who enjoyed discussing their ideas and experiences.

Should I work fulltime? In that case I would be able to finance a car, a social life, and maybe even my own apartment. For the first time in my life, I'd feel grown-up and independent. At the same time, challenging, good-paying fulltime jobs are usually offered to people with experience or education or both. The kind of job I'd likely be offered wouldn't promise much of a future.

As the cold, gray January of my senior year arrived, so did all these anxieties that I should have anticipated earlier.

Exercise 2-6   Writing a Paragraph in Context

INSTRUCTIONS: Supply the missing paragraph for the following composition. Write a rough draft and revise it before writing your paragraph in the space provided.

COMFORTABLE HOME

I'm twenty years old. While attending college I'm lucky enough to live with my parents and brother and sister in a very comfortable two-story home. There are several features of the house that I find very comfortable.

First, my bedroom provides me quite a bit of space; it's twelve by fifteen feet. A waterbed takes up much of one side of the room, and opposite the bed is a picture window that allows me to look out on an apple orchard and flower garden. Under the picture window I've located my stereo components. After school or work, I often listen to hard rock as I stretch out on my bed. As I lie in bed, I can enjoy watching a nineteen-inch color television with cable attached that stands in the right-hand corner of the room. I often enjoy retreating to my room to enjoy a beer and a movie in private.

Our kitchen is very comfortable, too. Twenty by seventeen feet, it contains a twenty cubic feet refrigerator stocked with cold beer, fresh meats, fruits, and vegetables. A round, oak kitchen table, about eight feet in diameter allows the whole family and friends to eat, drink, joke, and even discuss problems comfortably and securely. On the kitchen counter across from the table rests a twelve-inch color television—just in case an important baseball, basketball or football game is being broadcast. The gold and rust colors make the spacious room seem warm and friendly.

I've saved the best till last. My truly favorite room is the family room.

_____

_____

_____

_____

_____

_____

_____

_____

_____

_____

_____

_____

_____

_____

_____

_____

_____

_____

_____

_____

_____

_____

So you can see why I don't need to go "out" to enjoy myself. I've been very fortunate.

NAME _____

Exercise 2-7 Writing a Paragraph in Context

INSTRUCTIONS: Supply the missing paragraph for the following composition. Write a rough draft and revise it before writing your paragraph in the space provided.

AN IDEAL COUPLE

My friends Les and Mary seem to be a perfect couple. I met them in algebra class during my first semester at college. We became friends: we studied together, attended the same parties, went to the movies together, and bowled together. I've known them for a couple of years now, and the more I see them, the more I admire how they bring out the best in one another.

At parties, for example, while others try to impress everyone else, Les and Mary seem simply to enjoy being at the party together. I've noticed Les—without being asked or ordered to—serve Mary food or a drink; and I've also seen Mary do the same for Les. They seem to enjoy talking together about school, work, friends, and what they've been thinking about. They're always the ones seated together smiling and talking. They also manage to include others in their conversation, as well as in their eating and drinking. So while others seem to try to impress some guests at the expense of others, Les and Mary seem to make everyone as happy as they are.

I've also been with them when they are having a disagreement. Even then they seem to treat one another with respect.

_____

_____

_____

_____

_____

_____

_____

_____

_____

_____

_____

_____

_____

_____

_____

_____

_____

_____

_____

And they also manage to work well together, without bossing one another around or trying to get the other to do his or her work. When I helped Mary and Les prepare a celebration for his parents' twenty-fifth wedding anniversary, I observed that they not only accomplished a lot of work, they also enjoyed working with one another. After Les and Mary put up tables and chairs and cut the grass, they prepared sandwiches together for a hundred people. Each seemed to know what task needed to be done next and how to get it done. While working, they chatted and joked, rewarding themselves with a swallow of beer each time they finished making a sandwich or setting up a chair.

I wouldn't mind meeting someone like Mary. I guess that means I should become more like Les.

WRITING A PARAGRAPH'S SUPPORTING POINTS

Part of the process of writing and thinking through your ideas and gut reactions is to break those reactions down into separate supporting points. If your idea is complex, those supporting points may then provide you with the opportunity to question your gut reaction even further. Still, without this first break down (or analysis) of your own topic, no further thinking about the topic is possible.

In English class you may, for example, blurt out that your job is the worst job ever thought up by the mind of an employer. Then, your English instructor (being an English instructor) dares you to explain what you mean and prove your point. "That's easy!" you reply:

The pay's lousy, the customers are a pain in the neck, and the boss is always on my back.

In this way you have already thought up your paragraph's main supporting points. All ("All," he says?) that is left to do is to turn them into sentences and to draw out their details. Such reactions can usually be turned into clearer supporting points by making their conversational wording more specific.

"The pay's lousy" becomes "I don't make very much money," followed by details of how much money you do make and why you don't consider it "very much":

I don't make very much money. I usually take home about fifty dollars a week. That's just enough to pay the installment on my car loan and my car insurance.

"The customers are a pain in the neck" becomes "Most customers don't treat me very respectfully," followed by details of how customers have acted toward you:

Most customers don't treat me very respectfully. They usually throw their money at me instead of handing it to me, and it is not at all unusual for a customer to call me "Hey you!" or "Yo!"

"The boss is always on my back" becomes "The boss constantly presses me to do more and more work," followed by an example of the extra work he has asked you to do and how he has gone about "pressing" you to do it:

The boss constantly presses me to do more and more work. Last Tuesday night, I worked fifteen minutes extra. On Thursday night he remarked:

"It won't be any problem for you to stay an extra half-hour to help out, will it?"

For the exercises that follow, you are given a topic to be explained, one supporting point in a sentence with a sentence stating a follow-up detail, and two ideas for other supporting points. Your task is to turn each supporting idea into a sentence. Then follow it with a follow-up detail sentence that relates where your supporting point came from. Finally, think up your own supporting point and follow-up details for "Supporting point 4." Here's an example:

Topic to be explained:	Rose was very sick.
Supporting point 1:	She looked as if she were freezing.
Follow-up detail 1:	She covered herself from her chin to her toes with four woolen blankets.
Supporting point 2:	looked awful
	_____
	_____
Follow-up detail 2:	_____
	_____
Supporting point 3:	wouldn't eat
	_____
	_____
Follow-up detail 3:	_____
	_____
Supporting point 4:	_____
	_____
Follow-up detail 4:	_____
	_____

When written out and revised this might become:

(1) Rose was very sick. She looked as if she were freezing. She was covered from her chin to her toes with four woolen blankets. (2) Her appearance was frightening. Her teeth rattled while beads of sweat formed on her forehead. (3) She hadn't eaten anything nourishing the entire day. She had been so weak that all she could eat was a few spoonfuls of chicken broth. (4) She complained that she couldn't see well. She said that spots in front of her eyes prevented her from focusing.

Finally, you could add *first* or *second* wherever they seem natural, as well as phrases like *in addition* or the word *also*. But the main reason your sentences should stick together, or cohere, is that you have broken down your topic into supporting points explained further by follow-up details.

Follow this same procedure for the following exercises. After you've roughed out and revised your paragraph on a separate sheet of paper, read the versions to a couple of your fellow students to see how some sentences explain the paragraph's topic better than others do. Then write your paragraph in the space provided.

Exercise 2-8   Writing Supporting Points

INSTRUCTIONS: Develop a paragraph by writing sentences for each of the supporting points and follow-up details below. On a separate sheet of paper write a rough draft and revise it before writing your paragraph in the space provided.

1. Topic to be explained: The English teacher's behavior in class was stranger than usual.

   Supporting point 1:   First of all, he was sleeping in class.

   Follow-up detail 1:   As the students entered the classroom he was bent over his desk snoring away.

   Supporting point 2:   he was singing

   _____

   _____

   Follow-up detail 2:   _____

   _____

   Supporting point 3:   he was shouting

   _____

   _____

   Follow-up detail 3:   _____

   _____

   Supporting point 4:   _____

   _____

Follow-up detail 4: _____

_____

2. Your paragraph:

_____

_____

_____

_____

_____

_____

_____

_____

_____

_____

_____

_____

_____

_____

_____

_____

Exercise 2-9   Writing Supporting Points

INSTRUCTIONS: Develop a paragraph by writing sentences for each of the supporting points and details below. On a separate sheet of paper, write a rough draft and revise it before writing your paragraph in the space provided.

1. Topic to be explained: Ted was the most remarkable friend I ever had.

    Supporting point 1:   For one thing, Ted was always generous with his money.

    Follow-up detail 1:   Once when my car insurance was due, he lent me six hundred dollars.

    Supporting point 2:   supportive

    _____

    _____

    Follow-up detail 2:   _____

    _____

    Supporting point 3:   respectful

    _____

    _____

    Follow-up detail 3:   _____

    _____

    Supporting point 4:   _____

    _____

Follow-up detail 4: _____

_____

2. Your paragraph:

_____

_____

_____

_____

_____

_____

_____

_____

_____

_____

_____

_____

_____

_____

_____

_____

_____

_____

Exercise 2-10   Writing Supporting Points

INSTRUCTIONS: Develop a paragraph by writing sentences for each of the supporting points and details below. On a separate sheet of paper, write a rough draft and revise it before writing your paragraph in the space provided.

1. Topic to be explained: `The summer sale at the mall was better than I had expected.`

   Supporting point 1:   `Department stores had great sales on women's/men's clothes.`

   Follow-up detail 1:   `At Macy's, summer blouses/ shirts were marked down fifty percent.`

   Supporting point 2:   `fast food restaurants`

   _____

   _____

   Follow-up detail 2:   _____

   _____

   Supporting point 3:   `sporting goods stores`

   _____

   _____

   Follow-up detail 3:   _____

   _____

   Supporting point 4:   _____

   _____

Follow-up detail 4: _____

_____

2. Your paragraph:

_____

_____

_____

_____

_____

_____

_____

_____

_____

_____

_____

_____

_____

_____

_____

_____

_____

Exercise 2-11   Writing Supporting Points

INSTRUCTIONS: Develop a paragraph by writing sentences for each of the supporting points and details below. On a separate sheet of paper, write a rough draft and revise it before writing your paragraph in the space provided.

1. Topic to be explained: The Fourth of July has always been one of my favorite holidays.

   Supporting point 1:   I get to see members of my family I haven't seen since the previous year.

   Follow-up detail 1:   My aunt and uncle from South Carolina attend as well as my favorite sister who lives in Houston.

   Supporting point 2:   food

                         _____

                         _____

   Follow-up detail 2:   _____

                         _____

   Supporting point 3:   fun and games

                         _____

                         _____

   Follow-up detail 3:   _____

                         _____

Supporting point 4: _____

_____

Follow-up detail 4: _____

_____

2. Your paragraph:

_____

_____

_____

_____

_____

_____

_____

_____

_____

_____

_____

_____

_____

_____

_____

_____

_____

_____

Exercise 2-12   Writing Supporting Points

INSTRUCTIONS: Develop a paragraph by writing sentences for each of the supporting points and details below. On a separate sheet of paper, write a rough draft and revise it before writing your paragraph in the space provided.

1. Topic to be explained:
The ride on the New Jersey Transit bus was especially frustrating this morning.

Supporting point 1:
I never did manage to get a seat.

Follow-up detail 1:
I stood, holding on to the edge of someone else's seat, for the entire forty—minute trip.

Supporting point 2:
passengers

_____

_____

Follow-up detail 2:
_____

_____

Supporting point 3:
driver

_____

_____

Follow-up detail 3:
_____

_____

Supporting point 4:
_____

_____

Follow-up detail 4: _____

_____

2. Your paragraph:

_____

_____

_____

_____

_____

_____

_____

_____

_____

_____

_____

_____

_____

_____

_____

_____

_____

Exercise 2-13   Writing Supporting Points

INSTRUCTIONS: Develop a paragraph by writing sentences for each of the supporting points and details below. On a separate sheet of paper, write a rough draft and revise it before writing your paragraph in the space provided.

1. Topic to be explained: `Saturday afternoon I kept myself very busy working in our backyard.`

  Supporting point 1:   `First I cleaned up the mess alongside the garage.`

  Follow-up detail 1:   `I took the old tires to the dump and gave all the scrap wood to a neighbor.`

  Supporting point 2:   `leaves`

    _____

    _____

  Follow-up detail 2:   _____

    _____

  Supporting point 3:   `shrubbery`

    _____

    _____

  Follow-up detail 3:   _____

    _____

  Supporting point 4:   _____

    _____

Follow-up detail 4: _____

_____

2. Your paragraph:

_____

_____

_____

_____

_____

_____

_____

_____

_____

_____

_____

_____

_____

_____

_____

_____

_____

Exercise 2-14   Writing Supporting Points

INSTRUCTIONS: Develop a paragraph by writing sentences for each of the supporting points and details below. On a separate sheet of paper, write a rough draft and revise it before writing your paragraph in the space provided.

1. Topic to be explained: `Ed decided to buy a puppy for his eight-year-old daughter Edna.`

Supporting point 1:   `First, Ed thought Edna should be rewarded for having done so well in school.`

Follow-up detail 1:   `She had gotten four A's and two B's on her report card.`

Supporting point 2:   `no pet`

_____

_____

Follow-up detail 2:   _____

_____

Supporting point 3:   `no playmates`

_____

_____

Follow-up detail 3:   _____

_____

Supporting point 4:   _____

_____

Follow-up detail 4: _____

_____

2. Your paragraph:

_____

_____

_____

_____

_____

_____

_____

_____

_____

_____

_____

_____

_____

_____

_____

_____

_____

_____

_____

Exercise 2-15 Writing Supporting Points

INSTRUCTIONS: Develop a paragraph by writing sentences for each of the supporting points and details below. On a separate sheet of paper, write a rough draft and revise it before writing your paragraph in the space provided.

1. Topic to be explained: `It was very difficult to keep Mother and Father from discovering our plans to throw them a surprise anniversary party.`

  Supporting point 1: `They found notes we thought we had hidden away.`

  Follow-up detail 1: `For example they came across a guest list stuck in a telephone directory.`

  Supporting point 2: `phone calls`

  _____

  _____

  Follow-up detail 2: _____

  _____

  Supporting point 3: `supplies`

  _____

  _____

  Follow-up detail 3: _____

  _____

INSTRUCTIONAL SERVICE CENTER

Supporting point 4: _____

_____

Follow-up detail 4: _____

_____

2. Your paragraph:

_____

_____

_____

_____

_____

_____

_____

_____

_____

_____

_____

_____

_____

_____

_____

_____

Exercise 2-16   Writing Supporting Points

INSTRUCTIONS: Develop a paragraph by writing sentences for each of the supporting points and details below. On a separate sheet of paper, write a rough draft and revise it before writing your paragraph in the space provided.

1. Topic to be explained:

Tom begged the loan officer at People's Bank to lend him fifteen thousand dollars.

Supporting point 1:

He became very emotional, almost hysterical.

Follow-up detail 1:

Tears streamed down his cheeks as he described the kind of house he had always wanted to buy in the town where he had always wanted to live.

Supporting point 2:

job

_____

_____

Follow-up detail 2:

_____

_____

Supporting point 3:

collateral

_____

_____

Follow-up detail 3:

_____

_____

Supporting point 4: _____

_____

Follow-up detail 4: _____

_____

2. Your paragraph:

_____

_____

_____

_____

_____

_____

_____

_____

_____

_____

_____

_____

_____

_____

_____

_____

_____

Exercise 2-17   Writing Supporting Points

INSTRUCTIONS: Develop a paragraph by writing sentences for each of the supporting points and details below. On a separate sheet of paper, write a rough draft and revise it before writing your paragraph in the space provided.

1. Topic to be explained: `My eighty-year-old grandmother is one of the most independent people I have ever met.`

   Supporting point 1:   `She loves to travel, especially by herself.`

   Follow-up detail 1:   `Last summer she drove from Philadelphia to San Francisco--alone.`

   Supporting point 2:   `house`

   _____

   _____

   Follow-up detail 2:   _____

   _____

   Supporting point 3:   `car`

   _____

   _____

   Follow-up detail 3:   _____

   Supporting point 4:   _____

   _____

Follow-up detail 4: _____

_____

2. Your paragraph:

_____

_____

_____

_____

_____

_____

_____

_____

_____

_____

_____

_____

_____

_____

_____

_____

_____

Exercise 2-18 Writing a Paragraph with Supporting Points

INSTRUCTIONS: Using the given sentence as a topic sentence, write three supporting points, each with its own follow-up detail sentence.

1.   Although it's only the first week of March, spring seems to be arriving already.

_____

_____

_____

_____

_____

_____

_____

_____

_____

_____

_____

_____

_____

_____

_____

_____

_____

2. Miguel plans to be a much more serious student this semester.

_____

_____

_____

_____

_____

_____

_____

_____

_____

_____

_____

_____

_____

_____

_____

_____

_____

_____

Exercise 2-19 Writing a Paragraph with Supporting Points

INSTRUCTIONS: Using the given sentence as a topic sentence, write three supporting points, each with its own follow-up detail sentence.

1. *On Fire in Paradise* is just the kind of novel that romantic Irene loves to read.

_____

_____

_____

_____

_____

_____

_____

_____

_____

_____

_____

_____

_____

_____

_____

_____

_____

2.   Although his friends weren't going to like to hear it, Randy was going to tell them that he didn't want to go duck hunting with them anymore.

_____

_____

_____

_____

_____

_____

_____

_____

_____

_____

_____

_____

_____

_____

_____

_____

_____

Exercise 2-20   Writing a Paragraph with Supporting Points

INSTRUCTIONS: Using the given sentence as a topic sentence, write three supporting points, each with its own follow-up detail sentence.

1.   Just turned sixty, Theo felt better than he had in quite a long while.

_____

_____

_____

_____

_____

_____

_____

_____

_____

_____

_____

_____

_____

_____

_____

_____

_____

2. Charlotte and Charles were the most noticeable couple in the wedding party.

_____

_____

_____

_____

_____

_____

_____

_____

_____

_____

_____

_____

_____

_____

_____

_____

_____

WRITING A PARAGRAPH'S FOLLOW-UP DETAILS

When you've relaxed yourself enough to come up with a few points to help explain your paragraph's major point, or topic, the next step is to explain them further with follow-up details. They too will come to mind if you will reread and think about the implications of the words you've put together as your major supporting points.

For example, if your paragraph is explaining how to change the oil in your car by stating that one of the steps is to remove the old oil, it would be natural to tell the reader how such a task would be accomplished. Or, if your paragraph is explaining why you need to buy yourself some clothes, you might explain further what you mean when you say that you "have nothing to wear to school." You might describe what clothes you do wear to school and why you are not comfortable wearing them.

In the paragraphs that follow you are provided with a title, an opening sentence or two that tells you what the paragraph is intended to explain, and major supporting points. Your job is to see how these points work together to explain the paragraph's topic, and, following the directions in parentheses, follow up each major point with a sentence or two of supporting details.

Here's an example of a paragraph and how one student went about explaining why she thought Harry from "Zelda Decides to Marry Harry" was so good-looking:

> **Although Harry had asked Zelda to marry him six or seven times during their ten years of dating, last week Zelda finally agreed, for a few reasons. First, Harry's not bad looking. (Write a sentence or two describing Harry's good looks.) (1) <u>He's about six feet, two inches tall, a trim one hundred seventy pounds, with a slim waist and well developed chest. She says he reminds her of Billy Dee Williams</u>.**

Compare your results with those of a friend or two, or, take turns reading one another's paragraph aloud to hear whose version better develops the paragraph's main points.

Exercise 2-21   Writing Follow-up Details

INSTRUCTIONS: Write sentences as directed to add follow-up details for each of the main points in the paragraph below.

ZELDA DECIDES TO MARRY HARRY

   Although Harry had asked Zelda to marry him six or seven times during their ten years of dating, last week Zelda finally agreed for a few reasons. First, Harry's not bad looking. (Write a sentence or two describing Harry's good looks.)

(1) _____

_____

_____

_____

_____

_____

Second, he makes pretty good money and it looks as if, in a year or two, he'll earn even more. (Write a sentence or two stating what you consider "pretty good money," how he earns it, and what will happen to cause him to make more.)

(2) _____

_____

_____

_____

_____

_____

_____

Third, over the past ten years she's come to admire the way Harry treats his mother. (Write a sentence or two relating some admirable actions of Harry toward his mother.)

(3) _____

_____

_____

_____

_____

_____

Having thought about all these reasons for marrying Harry, Zelda could no longer remember why she had refused him the past six or seven times. This time she knew what she wanted.

Exercise 2-22 Writing Follow-up Details

INSTRUCTIONS: Write sentences as directed to add follow-up details for each of the main points in the paragraph below.

MAKING A HAMBURGER

To make a tasty hamburger requires only a few simple steps. First, combine the necessary ingredients in a bowl. (Write a sentence or two stating what ingredients you combine and how you go about combining them.)

(1) _____

_____

_____

_____

_____

_____

Next, shape the meat into patties. (Write a sentence or two explaining how you shape the meat into patties.)

(2) _____

_____

_____

_____

_____

_____

Broil the patties on the grill. (Write a sentence or two telling how to broil the patties on the grill.)

(3) _____

_____

_____

_____

_____

_____

Exercise 2-23   Writing Follow-up Details

INSTRUCTIONS: Write sentences as directed to add follow-up details for each of the main points in the paragraph below.

MY WORST DATE

My first date with Ernie/Sharon had to be my last: I was much too humiliated to dare to see him/her again. I embarrassed myself the first time when he/she picked me up. As I entered the living room, he/she was making conversation with my parents. (Write a sentence or two stating what you did or said or how you appeared in the living room that embarrassed you.)

(1) _____

_____

_____

_____

_____

_____

Ernie/Sharon treated me to dinner at the expensive Captain's Table. During dinner, in front of everyone in the restaurant (especially Ernie/Sharon), I made a fool of myself again. (Write a sentence or two relating what you did to make a fool of yourself in the restaurant and how you knew you had done this "in front of everyone.")

(2) _____

_____

_____

_____

_____

_____

_____

At the end of this very long, trying, and tiring evening, when Ernie/
Sharon parked his/her car in front of my house, I thought to myself,
"Finally, I'm home; my evening of humiliating myself is over." I was
wrong. (Write a sentence explaining how you managed, in the privacy of
Ernie's/Sharon's car parked in front of your own home, to embarrass
yourself.)

(3) _____

_____

_____

_____

_____

_____

So you see why I never had the courage to face Ernie/Sharon again.

Exercise 2-24   Writing Follow-up Details

INSTRUCTIONS: Write sentences as directed to add follow-up details for each of the main points in the paragraph below.

AN ANNOYING CLASSMATE

I hate to use the word, but Arnold, who sits next to me in composition class, is really annoying. For one thing, he interferes with the teacher's teaching. The other day, for example, while our instructor Ms. MacTavish was pointing out the strong and weak points of a composition by means of an overhead projector, Arnold acted his usual embarrassing self. (Write a sentence or two relating what Arnold did to embarrass Ms. MacTavish.)

(1) _____

_____

_____

_____

_____

_____

And he's certainly no more respectful of his fellow students than he is of his instructor. (Write a sentence or two relating what Arnold did to make fools out of his fellow students.)

(2) _____

_____

_____

_____

_____

_____

_____

And as if that weren't enough, the way he looks, smells, and sounds is particularly offensive to me, since I sit right next to him. (Write a sentence or two that describe Arnold's offensive appearance, smell, or sounds.)

(3) _____

_____

_____

_____

_____

_____

I'm really working hard to improve my writing, not because I don't want to take another writing course but because I don't want to take the same course with Arnold.

Exercise 2-25   Writing Follow-up Details

INSTRUCTIONS: Write sentences as directed to add follow-up details for each of the main points in the paragraph below.

THE UGLY OUTFIT

Last Wednesday evening, my new boy friend Hank arrived at my apartment to take me to dinner for my twenty-first birthday. As he stood in the doorway, I could not help but stare at the way he was dressed. I had not ever seen a sport coat like the one he was "sporting." (Write a sentence or two describing what about the sport coat caused the writer to "stare.")

(1) _____

_____

_____

_____

_____

_____

And you would never guess that the color or cut of the pants he was wearing was supposed to be worn with that sport coat. (Write a sentence or two describing what the pants looked like and how they clashed with the coat.)

(2) _____

_____

_____

_____

_____

_____

_____

But it was the shirt-tie combination that really made me speechless. (Write a sentence or two describing what about the shirt and tie made it difficult for the writer to speak.)

(3) _____

_____

_____

_____

_____

_____

I finally found the voice to tell Hank that we'd have pizza delivered for my twenty-first birthday.

Exercise 2-26   Writing Follow-up Details

INSTRUCTIONS: Write sentences as directed to add follow-up details for each of the main points in the paragraph below.

A TALENTED TEACHER

    Mr. Samuels, my eighth-grade teacher, was the most talented teacher I've had during my fourteen years of school. First of all, he treated all his students as adults except for those who acted younger than their years. (Write a sentence or two relating what Mr. Samuels did to show his students that he considered them mature human beings who were capable of helping themselves learn.)

(1) _____

_____

_____

_____

_____

_____

Second, Mr. Samuels, who taught us science, didn't just know facts and figures; he knew how to help us discover for ourselves what the facts and figures meant. (Write a sentence or two explaining how Mr. Samuels helped you think about the meaning of a scientific fact you studied.)

(2) _____

_____

_____

_____

_____

_____

_____

Most importantly, Mr. Samuels was very patient. (Write a sentence or two relating how Mr. Samuels was able to handle the same kinds of problems everyday.)

(3) _____

_____

_____

_____

_____

_____

Exercise 2-27   Writing Follow-up Details

INSTRUCTIONS: Write sentences as directed to add follow-up details for each of the main points in the paragraph below.

THERE'LL BE SOME CHANGES MADE

I have to admit that if I ever decide to marry I'm going to have to change the way I act. A spouse with any self-respect could never tolerate my bossiness. I'm a person who thinks he (or she) knows how to do things best. (Write a sentence or two relating how you've bossed someone around while he or she was performing a simple task.)

(1) _____

_____

_____

_____

_____

_____

Also, I'm cheap; I wouldn't spend a dollar if I could avoid it—especially not on someone else. (Write a sentence or two relating how you are cheap, even with your friends.)

(2) _____

_____

_____

_____

_____

_____

_____

Although everything has to be done my way, it's also true that I'm lazy.
(Write a sentence or two relating examples of laziness that a spouse
would be a fool to tolerate.)

(3) _____

_____

_____

_____

_____

_____

Exercise 2-28 Writing Follow-up Details

INSTRUCTIONS: Write sentences as directed to add follow-up details for each of the main points in the paragraph below.

VIRTUES OF EXERCISING

Ever since I've started swimming every day during my lunch hour, I've noticed a big change in the way I look and feel. First of all, I feel more energetic during the day. (Write a detailed sentence or two about a demanding task that you weren't able to perform before you began your exercise routine.)

(1) ___

___

___

___

___

___

Friends tell me I look much better too. (Write a detailed sentence or two that describes what about your appearance has caused your friends to tell you you look better.)

(2) ___

___

___

___

_____

_____

Finally, I don't seem to get depressed as much as I did before I began exercising. (Write a detailed sentence or two relating how daily worries don't seem to affect you as much as they did before you began exercising daily.)

(3) _____

_____

_____

_____

_____

_____

_____

REVISING A PARAGRAPH'S FOLLOW-UP DETAILS

The writer of each following paragraph needs to revise the paragraphs for one major problem: one of the major supporting points in each paragraph is NOT supported by a sentence of follow-up details.

For example, in the paragraph "My Favorite Holiday," the writer neglects to explain how food contributes to the festivity of his favorite holiday. He simply says that the "quality and variety are not to be believed." At this point his writing partner could help him by reading carefully to discover this weak spot in his explanation and then ask him questions about the very words he's used in his sentence:

Question 1: What about the "quality" of the food is so "unbelievable"?

Question 2: What about the "variety" of the food is so "unbelievable"?

This should lead the writer to answers that might very well follow up his unsupported point, such as:

Answer 1: Tenderloin steaks, home-made pasta, home-grown corn, and fresh shrimp are just some of the foods contributed by the picnickers.

Answer 2: Foods of many nations are served: Chinese vegetables, tacos and tortillas, and broiled spare ribs.

(Be sure to think up two of your own detail-sentences.)

Read each of the following paragraphs and underline the supporting point that hasn't been explained to the extent that the other supporting points have. Write out two questions about the undeveloped supporting point. Make sure that your questions contain the very words the writer uses in his sentences. Finally, write sentences to answer your questions that help explain the unsupported point.

Exercise 2-29   Revising Follow-up Details

INSTRUCTIONS: In the paragraph below, underline the supporting point that needs follow-up details, write two questions about the supporting point, and answer your questions with sentences of follow-up details.

MY FAVORITE HOLIDAY

The Fourth of July has always been one of my favorite holidays. First, I enjoy playing sports with my family and friends. After our family and friends play softball in a field behind our house, we all cool off in our next-door neighbor's pool. If there's time, we usually manage to play an hour or so of volleyball. Another pleasurable aspect of our Fourth-of-July celebrations is the food prepared by family and friends. The quality and variety is not to be believed. We all attend a spectacular fireworks display at the local firehouse. For two solid hours, all kinds of colors and shapes light up the sky, including an outline of the American flag. I wouldn't miss our Fourth-of-July celebration for anything.

Question 1: _____

_____

_____

_____

Question 2: _____

_____

_____

_____

Answer 1: _____

_____

_____

_____

_____

Answer 2: _____

_____

_____

_____

_____

Exercise 2-30   Revising Follow-up Details

INSTRUCTIONS: In the paragraph below, underline the supporting point that needs follow-up details, write two questions about the supporting point, and answer your questions with sentences of follow-up details.

THE GENEROUS HOSTESS

Maureen hosted a Memorial Day barbecue in her backyard, and she included some wonderful surprises. First of all, the food she served was not what you'd usually be offered at a picnic-barbecue. Broiled salmon steaks, artichoke hearts, lobster, and squid were spread out on the picnic table. In addition, music was provided. Roving violinists played whatever songs you requested while in her ample basement a rock-band blared its sounds for the more contemporary. Maureen also presented gifts to her guests. All Maureen's guests hoped they would be invited to her next party.

Question 1: _____

_____

_____

_____

Question 2: _____

_____

_____

_____

Answer 1: _____

_____

_____

_____

_____

Answer 2: _____

_____

_____

_____

Exercise 2-31   Revising Follow-up Details

INSTRUCTIONS: In the paragraph below, underline the supporting point that needs follow-up details, write two questions about the supporting point, and answer your questions with sentences of follow-up details.

THE INTERVIEW

    After her interview at Acme, Inc., Elza was pleased with the impression she had made on Mr. Juarez. She made very sure that she greeted him properly. When he introduced himself, she smiled self-confidently and extended her hand to be shaken. "I'm very happy to meet you, Mr. Juarez," she said, remembering her friend's advice that she should make eye contact and use his name. When he asked whether she had ever worked as a cashier before, she answered in great detail. Also, Mr. Juarez seemed to enjoy talking to her. He asked her how her studies were going and when she expected to be awarded her associate's degree in accounting. They chatted at least twenty minutes past the time Mr. Juarez had spent with the candidates he had interviewed before her. When Elza left his office, her hopes were very high.

Question 1: _____

_____

_____

_____

_____

Question 2: _____

_____

_____

_____

_____

Answer 1: _____

_____

_____

_____

_____

Answer 2: _____

_____

_____

_____

Exercise 2-32   Revising Follow-up Details

INSTRUCTIONS: In the paragraph below, underline the supporting point that needs follow-up details, write two questions about the supporting point, and answer your questions with sentences of follow-up details.

MARTHA'S DRIVING TEST

Martha was quite nervous while taking her driver's exam. She had left her glasses at home, so she couldn't make out the letters and words she was reading. She focused so hard trying to make out what they were, that she gave herself a headache and felt a bit sick to her stomach. The state troopers patrolling the exam room also bothered her a great deal. To make matters worse, she couldn't prevent herself from recalling the two times she had already failed this test, which distracted her even more. She remembered the time last December she had done Christmas shopping rather than studying for the test, so she failed. Then she recalled how the following March she had studied distances, speeds, and penalties so much that she mixed them all up when she took the test, and failed again. So it came as no surprise to her that she was worried about passing it this time.

Question 1: _____

_____

_____

_____

Question 2: _____

_____

_____

_____

Answer 1: _____

_____

_____

_____

_____

Answer 2: _____

_____

_____

_____

_____

Exercise 2-33   Revising Follow-up Details

INSTRUCTIONS: In the paragraph below, underline the supporting point that needs follow-up details, write two questions about the supporting point, and answer your questions with sentences of follow-up details.

LEONA'S AFTERNOON AT THE BEACH

Leona's long-awaited afternoon at the beach was not what she had hoped for. The wind blew fiercely. It blew her straw hat right off her head into the Atlantic; it rumpled the pages of her novel every time she tried to read. The cool breeze also made her underestimate the strength of the sun on her fair skin. The waves were rough. Twice they ploughed up the beach to engulf Leona's blanket, books, and lunch. And finally they succeeded at carrying away her fifty-dollar straw hat. So Leona has promised herself to be more prepared for such possibilities the next time she goes to the beach.

Question 1: _____

_____

_____

_____

_____

Question 2: _____

_____

_____

_____

Answer 1: _____

_____

_____

_____

Answer 2: _____

_____

_____

_____

Exercise 2-34 Revising Follow-up Details

INSTRUCTIONS: In the paragraph below, underline the supporting point that needs follow-up details, write two questions about the supporting point, and answer your questions with sentences of follow-up details.

MY RELAXING-AT-HOME CLOTHES

When I come home from work, I put on a certain set of clothes that I find very comfortable—especially in the fall or winter. First of all, there's my gray sweatshirt. Made of cotton fleece softened further by innumerable washings, my oversized sweatshirt makes me feel both warm and free from the fitted blouse or dress I've worn all day. My six-year-old jeans feel good for similar reasons. The denim has been worn smooth and feels more like velvet than cotton. They fit my body like a comfortable second skin. Yet most crucial to my relaxing-at-home outfit is what I put on my feet the minute I step in the door.

Question 1: _____

_____

_____

_____

Question 2: _____

_____

_____

_____

Answer 1: _____

_____

_____

_____

_____

Answer 2: _____

_____

_____

_____

Exercise 2-35　Revising Follow-up Details

INSTRUCTIONS:　In the paragraph below, underline the supporting point that needs follow-up details, write two questions about the supporting point, and answer your questions with sentences of follow-up details.

A BAD INVESTMENT

　　A month ago Janet paid five hundred dollars for a 1965 Dodge Polara. It turned out to be a very bad investment. First, it costs a lot to keep it fueled. Although she drives it only to work and back (a round trip of about twenty miles), she finds herself at the gas station twice a week handing the attendant a ten-dollar bill. Also, the heater doesn't work properly. One cold, rainy evening after she had gotten off from work, Janet turned the heater switch on only to discover that the fan worked only when the car was in reverse. Unfortunately, too, Janet really didn't take a good look at the tires when she bought this "lemon."

Question 1: _____

_____

_____

_____

_____

Question 2: _____

_____

_____

_____

Answer 1: _____

_____

_____

_____

_____

Answer 2: _____

_____

_____

_____

_____

Exercise 2-36   Revising Follow-up Details

INSTRUCTIONS: In the paragraph below, underline the supporting point that needs follow-up details, write two questions about the supporting point, and answer your questions with sentences of follow-up details.

MY GREATEST WEAKNESS

I have to admit it: I always eat twice as much as I should. Take breakfast, for example; everyone else in my family eats two eggs, two slices of bacon, two slices of toast, and an eight-ounce glass of juice. Double these amounts and you'll have some idea of how much I eat for breakfast. At a party I eat and drink twice as much as everyone else. During the day, at work, my lunch and in-between snacks provide me with much more food than my co-workers seem to need. I consume a half-dozen jelly doughnuts during my 9:30 coffee break, eight to ten slices of cold pizza, a large container of popcorn, and a half-gallon of grape Kool-Aide. I know my health will suffer if I continue gorging myself like this, so I'd better do something soon—like switch to Diet Coke.

Questions 1: _____

_____

_____

_____

Question 2: _____

_____

_____

_____

Answer 1: _____

_____

_____

_____

Answer 2: _____

_____

_____

_____

REVISING TO IMPROVE PARAGRAPH LOGIC

Often when you are writing a rough draft, your thinking and the sentence you're writing may suddenly wander from, or merely rephrase, the point your topic sentence promised to explain. Usually such errors or repetitions have something to do with the subject of your paragraph, but they do not directly address or support the point you made in your topic sentence.

Such errors should pop out at you when you reread your rough drafts, especially if you read them aloud or ask someone else to read them aloud. Reading your paragraph should remind you of what you've set out to explain and how you're going about doing so. Any question that stands in the way of your explaining, any sentence that confuses you or slows down your reading temporarily is likely to be one of those that fails to follow up the thinking that went before it.

For example, notice how the underlined sentence below does not help explain the paragraph's topic, what Patricia imagined she would do with her lottery winnings:

> **Patricia imagined how she would spend her new million-dollar lottery winnings. She and her husband would spend the winter in Bermuda. She would buy her parents a house that wouldn't require them to walk up and down stairs. <u>She would be really excited when she finally received her first check.</u> Finally, she dreamed about sending all of her eight children to Oxford.**

Whether Patricia will be excited or not when she receives her check, or how that excitement will show up in her behavior, could be the topic of another paragraph about her having won the lottery. However, in contrast to the other sentences in this paragraph, it does not help explain further Patricia's fantasies about what she will do with the money.

In the following paragraphs, you will find one sentence that, more than the others, fails to develop the paragraph's topic. As you read each paragraph, this sentence may stop you in your tracks, since it does not offer the same kind of proof or explanation of the topic as the other sentences in the paragraph do. Underline the illogical sentence, and then write a sentence that does explain the topic further and provides the kind of proof evident in the other sentences.

For instance, in the preceding example paragraph you might replace the illogical sentence about how Patricia will be excited with one that, like the others in the paragraph, states another way that she imagines herself spending her winnings:

She pictured herself swimming in her own olympic-sized swimming pool.

Compare your solutions with those of a fellow student. Then try to improve your own.

Exercise 2-37   Improving Paragraph Logic

INSTRUCTIONS: In each paragraph below, underline the sentence that merely repeats or wanders from the topic being explained and then write a sentence that supports the topic.

1.   Eileen decided she wouldn't date Ed anymore. For one thing, last week he bragged to her about how many girlfriends he had had. She had also heard from her girlfriend Maria that Ed had been married twice. She had discovered too that Ed was just not the wonderful catch she thought he was. Finally, Ed had a terrible habit of never offering to pay his portion of the costs of their dates.

_____

_____

_____

2.   Tom enjoys his job as a cashier at MacDonald's very much. First, he makes twice as much money as he expected to. He really feels rich now that he's making more money than he thought he would. He has also begun dating Sheri, who works the register next to him. In addition, his supervisor has promised him a raise and a promotion within the next two months.

_____

_____

_____

3.   The shopping mall was very crowded this weekend. It took me ten minutes to find a parking place. Then I waited for twenty minutes to be waited on at MacDonald's. No matter where you went, there were people, people, people! I wasn't even able to get a seat at the afternoon movie!

_____

_____

_____

4. Although I love my family, they sometimes annoy me. My husband Al, for example, never helps with the house cleaning. None of them is at all generous as members of our family. My daughter Mary expects that her favorite jeans always be washed, dried, and ironed to her specifications. And every morning at 5 a.m., our dog, Fido, whines until I take him out for a walk.

_____

_____

_____

5. Manuel has learned a lot about being a student here at MCCC. For one, he now knows that he must read his assignments several times before going to class. He has promised himself that never again will he attend class without having prepared his assignments. He has also discovered that he must attend class in order to learn what the teacher is teaching. Finally, he now knows he should discuss what he's studying with other students in the class so he can find out what their ideas are.

_____

_____

_____

Exercise 2-38   Improving Paragraph Logic

INSTRUCTIONS In each paragraph below, underline the sentence that merely repeats or wanders from the topic being explained and then write a sentence that supports the topic.

1. Max always misbehaves in English class. For one thing, he usually throws spit balls at the teacher's back while he is writing on the blackboard. Sometimes too, he brings his lunch to class and hands out sandwiches, cookies, and apples to his classmates instead of doing his assignments. He's always doing things like that to make the teacher holler at him. Occasionally in the middle of class, while other students are writing, he shouts at the teacher, "I wouldn't do such a stupid assignment if my life depended on it."

    _____

    _____

    _____

    _____

    _____

2. Whenever she hosts a party, Jenny goes to a great deal of trouble to entertain her guests. Usually she hires a five-piece band that plays many different kinds of music. Generally, she offers her guests champagne and caviar laid out on the finest of china. For her guests, nothing is too good. She also pays for their rooms at a nearby motel if they're too tired to drive home by the end of the party.

    _____

    _____

    _____

    _____

    _____

3. While Mrs.Smith was away on vacation, her son Tommy really made a mess of her house. First, he threw a party for all his friends. Also, he left a week's worth of greasy, encrusted dishes on the floor in the television room. A friend of his slept in his mother's bed for the entire week, but never made it. Several dozen crushed beer cans stuck out from under the sofa and chairs in the living room.

_____

_____

_____

4. Yesterday was a day that proved Murphy's Law: if anything can go wrong it will. First, I had forgotten to set my alarm clock, so I was an hour late getting up for work. Second, on the way to work I had a terrible delay. Then, at work, while pouring fluid into the mimeo-machine container, I spilled some all over my new chino pants. Finally, an hour later, my boss informed me that the raise I had asked for was exorbitant and that I was fired.

_____

_____

_____

5. Frank is one of the laziest people I've ever met. Although he lives only two blocks from school, he drives there everyday. Frank says there's something wrong with his thyroid. Believe it or not, Frank will make himself miserable watching a television show he hates rather than get up from the couch to change the channel. Rather than unbutton it, he pulls his shirt up over his head when getting out of his clothes.

_____

_____

_____

MORE TOPICS FOR WRITING AND REVISING

The following topics are derived from openings of some very fine short stories by authors who have enriched the language you use every day in your socializing, thinking, and communicating. Read each passage to yourself. Then read it aloud as dramatically as possible. Try to hear and reproduce the tone you think the words suggest. When you come across a word or expression you don't undestand, try to narrow its meaning by thinking what kinds of meanings would make sense at that point in the sentence and paragraph. Discuss possibilities with your fellow students, and then think about the meanings offered in the dictionary.

To get yourself to think ever more closely about how the author may have written and revised the opening of his or her story, work through the exercises that follow it. The first question asks you to respond to the opening as a whole. How do the general remarks and details work together to give you a unified view of a situation or character? The second allows you to think about the author's words even more deeply by directing you to supply further complementary details. You become co-author. Third, you are asked to continue the story in whatever way you believe makes sense, given how the story begins. Read your passage and the continuation of it together, and decide if you've begun to make the story your own.

Finally, you are asked to make the jump to your own experience by writing and revising an explanation of a topic drawn from the situation set up in the opening of the story. In writing and revising your composition, your job is *not* to write about the opening of the story, but to write about an incident in your own life that the story opening suggests.

In revising your composition, apply the strategies of question and answer by reading your own rough draft and having your partner read it. This is the kind of assignment that will allow you to see, if you don't already, the intimate connection between reading and writing and how they feed off one another.

One last point. To see how the author developed and concluded his or her story, go to your library and look up a copy of the story. You may be surprised.

Exercise 2-39   Writing Topics

INSTRUCTIONS: Read the passage below, do the exercises that follow, and write and revise a composition on the given topic.

DEALING WITH OTHERS

Opening of Flannery O'Connor's "A Good Man Is Hard to Find" (taken from Flannery O'Connor, *A Good Man Is Hard to Find*, published by Harcourt, Brace, 1953).

The grandmother didn't want to go to Florida. [1]She wanted to visit some of her connections in east Tennessee and she was seizing at every chance to change Bailey's mind. [2]Bailey was the son she lived with, her only boy. He was sitting on the edge of his chair at the table, bent over the orange sports section of the *Journal*. [3]"Now look here, Bailey," she said, "see here, read this," and she stood with one hand on her thin hip and the other rattling the newspaper at his bald head. "Here this fellow that calls himself The Misfit is aloose from the Federal Pen and headed toward Florida and you read here what it says he did to these people. Just you read it. I wouldn't take my children in any direction with a criminal like that aloose in it. I couldn't answer to my conscience if I did."

Bailey didn't look up from his reading so she wheeled around then and faced the children's mother, a young woman in slacks, whose face was as broad and innocent as a cabbage and was tied around with a green head-kerchief that had two points on the top like rabbit's ears. [4]She was sitting on the sofa, feeding the baby his apricots out of a jar. "The children have been to Florida before," the old lady said. [5]"You all ought to take them somewhere else for a change so they would see different parts of the world and be broad. They never have been to east Tennessee. . . ."

1. The sights, sounds, and remarks in the opening of O'Connor's story work together to give you some idea of how the grandmother may treat other people, especially ones she knows well. In two or three sentences describe that treatment.

_____

_____

_____

_____

2. The numbers 1 to 5 in the excerpt you just read correspond to the directions below. Following these directions, compose sentences that develop the story's opening even further. Read your newly revised passage aloud to hear if the sentences you've written help your reader imagine this scene a little differently. The first one is done for you.

1) State what connections the grandmother wanted to visit and why.

She hadn't seen Lilah Mae, her second cousin

once removed, since Bailey was born.

2) Describe Bailey's appearance.

_____

_____

3) Quote what the newspaper said about The Misfit.

_____

_____

4) Relate how the baby was behaving.

_____

_____

5) Quote the grandmother explaining what about visiting east Tennessee would be "broadening."

_____

_____

3. Continue the story in any way you think fits in with the opening. Write for about five minutes. Do not pause for more than a few seconds at a time.

Exercise 2-39 Writing Topics (continued)

WRITING TOPIC

4. Write a composition about an incident when you wanted to do one thing and someone else (who perhaps had more power) wanted you to do another. Explain how the two of you negotiated your differences—or how you settled your differences in some other way. Use the questions below as guidelines.

   What made you want one thing and the other person another?

   How come you couldn't ignore the other person's wishes?

   What did you say or do to try to change the other person's mind?

   How did the other person react to your efforts to have things your way?

   Who won? How?

   _____

   _____

   _____

   _____

   _____

   _____

   _____

   _____

   _____

   _____

Exercise 2-40 Writing Topics

INSTRUCTIONS: Read the passage below, do the exercises that follow, and write and revise a composition on the given topic.

EFFECTS OF CHANGE

Opening of Nadine Gordimer's "The Train from Rhodesia" (taken from Nadine Gordimer, *The Soft Voice of the Serpent and Other Stories*, published by Viking Press, 1962).

[1]The train came out of the red horizon and bore down toward them over the single straight track.

[2]The stationmaster came out of his little brick station with its pointed chalet roof, feeling the creases in his serge uniform in his legs as well. [3]A stir of preparedness rippled through the squatting native vendors waiting in the dust; the face of a carved wooden animal, eternally surprised, stuck out of a sack. [4]The stationmaster's barefoot children wandered over. From the gray mud huts with the untidy heads that stood within a decorated mud wall, chickens, and dogs with their skin stretched like parchment over their bones, followed the piccanins down to the track. The flushed and perspiring west cast a reflection, faint, without heat, upon the station, upon the tin shed marked "Goods," upon the walled kraal, upon the gray tin house of the stationmaster and upon the sand, that lapped all around, from sky to sky, cast little rhythmical cups of shadow, so that the sand became the sea, and closed over the children's black feet softly and without imprint.

[5]The stationmaster's wife sat behind the mesh of her verandah. Above her head the hunk of a sheep's carcass moved slightly, dangling in a current of air.

They waited. . . .

1. The details in the opening passage of this story work together to provide the reader with an overall impression of this opening scene. Describe that impression in two or three sentences.

_____

_____

_____

_____

2. The numbers 1 to 5 in the excerpt you just read correspond to the directions below. Following these directions, compose sentences that develop the story's opening even further. Read your newly revised passage aloud to hear if it helps your reader imagine this scene a little differently. The first one is done for you.

1) Describe what the train looked like.

    `The sun reflected blindingly off the steel`

    `engine as it grew bigger and louder.`

2) Describe how the stationmaster presented himself.

    _____

    _____

3) Describe what the animal looked like.

    _____

    _____

4) Relate what the children did when they got to the track.

    _____

    _____

5) Relate what the wife did as she sat on the verandah.

    _____

    _____

3. Continue the story in any way you think fits in with the opening. Write for about five minutes. Try not to pause.

WRITING TOPIC

4. Some people like machines. Others don't. Most, however, find them useful, and few can avoid their having an effect on their lives. Write a composition explaining how a machine entered your life and how it altered your former way of living.

Exercise 2-41   Writing Topics

INSTRUCTIONS: Read the passage below, do the exercises that follow, and write and revise a composition on the given topic.

FIRST IMPRESSIONS

Opening of John Updike's "A & P" (taken from John Updike, *Pigeon Feathers and Other Stories*, published by Alfred A. Knopf, 1962).

In walks these three girls in nothing but bathing suits. [1]I'm in the third checkout slot, with my back to the door, so I don't see them until they're over by the bread. The one that caught my eye first was the one in the plaid green two-piece. [2]She was a chunky kid, with a good tan and a sweet broad softy-looking can with those two crescents of white just under it, where the sun never seems to hit, at the top of the backs of her legs. I stood there with my hand on a box of HiHo crackers trying to remember if I rang it up or not. [3]I ring it up again and the customer starts giving me hell. [4]She's one of these cash-register-watchers, a witch about fifty with rouge on her cheekbones and no eyebrows, and I know it made her day to trip me up. She's been watching cash registers for fifty years and probably never seen a mistake before.

By the time I got her feathers smoothed and her goodies into a bag—she gives me a little snort in passing, if she'd been born at the right time they would have burned her over in Salem—by the time I get her on her way the girls had circled around the bread and were coming back, without a pushcart, back my way along the counters, in the aisle between the checkouts and the Special bins. [5]They didn't even have shoes on. . . .

1. The opening passage of "A & P" presents you with the speaker's first impressions of people who have come into the store. In two or three sentences, state how the speaker tends to view people.

    _____

    _____

    _____

    _____

2. The numbers 1 to 5 in the excerpt you just read correspond to the directions below. Following these directions, compose sentences

that develop the story's opening even further. Read your newly revised passage aloud to hear if it helps your reader imagine this scene a little differently. The first one is done for you.

1) Relate what the girls are doing over by the bread.

   <u>One girl is whispering something to the girl</u>

   <u>next to her while the other is choosing</u>

   <u>between a Twinkie and a Devil Dog.</u>

2) Describe the "chunky kid's" face.

   _____

   _____

3) Relate what the customer said.

   _____

   _____

4) Relate how the customer made sure she wasn't cheated.

   _____

   _____

5) Describe what the other two girls were wearing.

   _____

   _____

3. Continue the story in any way you think fits in with the opening. Write for about five minutes. Try not to pause.

WRITING TOPIC

4. Recall when you first met someone you later got to know better. Write a composition explaining how you discovered that your first view of that person was inaccurate. How did the person appear, act, and talk when you first met him or her? Did he or she appear, act, and speak differently as you got to know him or her?

CHAPTER 3

SENTENCE LOGIC

As your revising focuses on smaller and smaller components of your rough draft, you will find yourself rereading and rethinking rough drafts of individual sentences to see if their points are made as clearly as possible. Questioning the meanings of confusing words and phrases is still the technique to use. As you make the logic of your paragraphs clearer to yourself and your reader, sentences that disturb that logic will become more and more obvious and annoying. Your writing and revising process—starting from writing down words freely, generating ideas from words, and "questioning" important ideas into explanatory paragraphs—is now focusing on the tool that makes such thinking and explaining possible: the *sentence*.

When you're reading through a paragraph and you've come upon a sentence that makes you lose the paragraph's line of thought, chances are there's something wrong with the word choice or word order of the sentence. (If the entire sentence has nothing at all in common with the paragraph's main idea or if it simply repeats a generalization already made, you're likely to question the relevance of the entire sentence.) Ask yourself or the writer questions about the words that confused you. Answering these questions will help you or the writer to improve the confusing word choice or word order. Then reread and revise it in the light of the rough draft you have already written.

Again, the more readers you work with to read and question your writing, the better the chances are that you'll discover what confusing words and word combinations need to be revised. Recall the rough draft on the overcoming-a-fear topic from Part 1:

> When my uncle asked me to join his job, I knew I had to face this situation of not climbing high off the ground. I just couldn't turn the job down, so I planned a way to get over it. I visited our local play ground twice a day, forcing myself to climb on the jungle gym.

Many readers, for example, would be stopped in their reading tracks when they reached the phrase "to join his job" in this example. From the point of view of more meaningful word choices, you might want to know just what "job" the writer had in mind. From the point of view of more usual word combinations, many readers would be confused in seeing the word *join* "joined" with the word *job*, at least in written explanations.

After having listened to a reader describe the confusion he suffers at this point in the sentence and having tried to answer questions produced by that confusion, the writer is now in a position to recall alternative words and word combinations. These new words and phrases should allow the reader to continue on his way through the sentence, and, ultimately, to relate it to all the others in the paragraph:

> **When my Uncle Ned asked me if I wanted to work for him as an apprentice in his roofing business, I jumped at the chance. He offered me ten dollars an hour to start, plus the opportunity to learn more technical and better-paying skills. There was one problem, however: I was terrified of being even a foot off the ground. Even climbing the stairs to my bedroom made my heart race.**

Notice from this revised paragraph how revising one sentence can stimulate and reorder your thinking in such a way that subsequent, confusing word choices and phrases—like "I knew I had to face this situation of not climbing high off the ground"—seem to be easier to spot and revise. At the same time, more relevant and imaginable circumstances—"He offered me ten dollars an hour to start." "Even climbing the stairs to my bedroom made my heart race."—may be triggered by reconsidering the meaning or placement of a word or phrase.

Improving word choice and phrasing is a matter of noticing that certain word combinations make sense when they're written together while others do not. "To join a job," for example, is a phrase that may work in spoken, colloquial, English but not in written, formal, English. The more readers you ask to read your rough drafts, the more you will become aware of such words and phrases that confuse and distract.

More extensive revising of confusing word combinations—revising whole phrases and sentences—is often best accomplished by rewriting the entire sentence "from scratch." When an entire sentence seems to contribute a relevant point to the paragraph's main idea but in a confusing way, rewrite the entire sentence, first by thinking up the most logical subject and verb and then by letting the words you choose as subjects and verbs generate further words.

To reconsider what the focal point of your sentence should be, its subject, think again about what you really wanted to make a point about in the sentence. Then name it as specifically as possible. For example, read the following rough draft of a sentence:

Rita got the job she wanted from the man who saw her in the personnel office.

The writer must decide whether she wants to make a point about "Rita" or "the man who saw her in the personnel office." Hence, the words used as the subject should be either "Rita" or "the personnel director," or perhaps "Mr. X who interviewed me."

Next, ask yourself what the named subject (in this case "Rita") has done or what physical or mental state she's in. (Has she *mailed* a letter, or *has* she *been* anxious?) Your answers to these questions will produce the verb of your sentence. The word you choose to be the verb of the sentence will allow you to make a point about the subject you've named. The verb, in other words, is what creates your point or idea. It's important to think of a verb that, as much as possible, allows your reader to imagine what you noted or observed. This observation (in life or in your reading) is often the basis for the conclusions your composition is meant to explain.

In the "Rita" sentence, for example, if you choose to make a point about Rita, you need to ask yourself what she did, what happened to her, or what state of mind or body she was in. Here are some possibilities:

Rita accepted. . . .
Rita needed. . . .
Rita was granted. . . .
Rita was offered. . . .
Rita was hired for. . . .

However, if you want to emphasize what the interviewer did, or what happened to him, or what state of mind or body he was in, you might come up with these possibilities, among others:

The personnel director offered Rita the job. . . .
The personnel director awarded Rita the job. . . .
The personnel director hired Rita for the position. . . .

Once you've straightened out what you want to name as your subject and what you want to say your subject did, the other words you need to complete your idea will follow. The meaning of the words you've chosen for the subject and verb, "The personnel director offered . . . ," for example, will lead you to the words you need to complete that idea. One possibility might be:

The personnel director offered Rita the data-entry position she had applied for.

Thus, once you've finally chosen the word you want to use as your verb, the words to complete the idea of the sentence will fall into place. These "completing" words are called *complements*.

Since the verb is the part of the sentence that allows you to say whatever you want about the subject, it stands to reason that if you make clearer the meaning of an already meaningful verb, your sentence will be even clearer. The type of word that allows you to accomplish this is the *adverb*. It is a word or group of words that "add" meaning to the verb. Adding adverbs to your sentence is the next step in rewriting a confusing sentence so that its meaning is clearer.

Some of your reader's questions that adverbs are meant to answer are:

1. *In what manner* did something happen?
2. *By what means* did something happen?
3. *When* did something happen?
4. *Where* did something happen?

In order to restructure your sentence draft further, ask yourself these questions about your sentence's verb, for example:

1. **In what manner** did the personnel director offer Rita the position?
   He offered it **with a hearty handshake**.

2. **By what means** did he offer her the position?
   He offered it to her **by slapping her on the back and shouting, "Welcome Aboard!"**

3. **When** did he offer it to her?
   He offered it to her **yesterday**.

4. **Where** did he offer Rita the job?
   The personnel director, Mr. Fidelis, offered her the job **in his office**.

The final improvement to help you rewrite a confusing sentence is by adding *adjectives*. An adjective is a word or combination of words that tells the reader something further about a noun. Sometimes a sentence may be unclear to a reader because a person, place, or thing that you've named—the noun (the word comes from the Latin word for name, *nomen*) is not worded as specifically as it might be. Read this sentence, for example:

The woman offered the man the position as a law clerk.

This sentence has two unspecified nouns: "man" and "woman." (The word "position" already has a phrase describing it.) Let's assume that we don't know the names or titles of this woman or man. We have to describe their appearance, putting into words (adjectives) as best we can what we observed. Here's one possibility:

The woman <u>wearing the blue pin-striped suit</u> offered the position <u>as law clerk</u> to the <u>balding, muscular</u> man <u>sitting on the other side of her huge oak desk.</u>

The points you've made in the earlier sentences of your paragraph will indicate what details you need to emphasize about the persons, places, and things you mention. For example, if a nursing student concludes that a patient may be suffering from a viral infection, he will probably explain this view by describing the changes in appearance and behavior that caused him to believe this.

As you recompose confusing sentences, if you find yourself (or another reader) asking questions like:

<u>Which one</u> or <u>what kind</u> of person, place or thing do you mean?

<u>How much</u> or <u>how many</u> persons, places, or things do you mean?

try to recall what you observed or read, and write it into your revised sentence:

<u>Which</u> woman?
The <u>thin</u> woman <u>wearing the blue pin-striped suit.</u>

<u>Which</u> man?
The <u>balding, muscular</u> man <u>sitting on the other side of the huge oak desk.</u>

<u>Which</u> position?
The position <u>as law clerk.</u>

To sum up, when you "hit" a sentence that doesn't seem to fit in with the line of thought you've been developing in the rest of the paragraph, reread the paragraph to make sure you've followed its line of thought correctly. Then rewrite the parts of the confusing sentence by asking and answering specific questions about the words in the sentence. If you revise your sentences in this way, you will begin to make better use in your writing of your daily listening, speaking, and reading.

The exercises in this section will help you use words you already know from your reading, speaking, and writing as effective parts of your sentences—words that perhaps you do not take full advantage of in your writing. But when you do begin to use them more effectively, you will find that each of your sentences will contribute a clearer point to the logic of your paragraphs.

COMBINING SUBJECTS AND VERBS

When you name a person, place, or thing in order to say something about it, you are using a noun as the subject of your sentence. The word or words that will allow you to say something about the subject is the verb. When revising first versions of especially confusing sentences, it is often necessary to let go of the words and word order you've used in your first version and to refocus your attention on renaming the subject of your sentence. In the following sentence, for example, the writer has lost track of his subject. Possibly he realizes this, even as he writes the sentence, so he can't afford to let the sentence end. It just runs out of energy. The reader loses track of what the writer wants to make a point about and what point he wants to make:

> **Her grandfather was sitting next to her telling the story she always liked in bed and the little girl fell asleep all of a sudden.**

This rough draft of a sentence can be "questioned" and revised in order to transform it into a clearer, more informative sentence. The questions to ask the writer should begin to lead him to naming more exactly what he wants to make a point about. Once he's done that, he can continue reconstructing the sentence by choosing a more meaningful verb:

> **"What do you want to make a point about?"**
> **"Laetitia."**
>
> **"What point do you want to make about her, that she fell asleep?"**
> **"No. I really wanted to emphasize the fact that she yawned."**

Having gotten this far, the writer can rewrite his sentence by renaming the subject and combining it with a more meaningful verb:

> **Four-year-old Laetitia yawned as her grandfather finished his second reading of "Goldilocks and the Three Bears."**

"Laetitia" is now named as the subject of the sentence, and the point that is made about her is the verb "yawned."

Exercise 3-1 Choosing Subjects

INSTRUCTIONS: In each sentence below, you are given a sentence whose subject has not been named. Think about what point is being made about the missing subject. Then write three subjects that might well have performed the action expressed in the sentence. The first one is done for you.

1.   Hurling the newspaper at the Smith's front porch, the _____ awoke the Smith's bloodhound which had been sleeping peacefully on the porch steps.

   1) paperboy   **2)** mailman   **3)** deliverygirl

2.   The _____ halted traffic at the intersection of Simmons and Main Street in order to investigate the accident that had just taken place there.

   1) _____   **2)** _____   **3)** _____

3.   Because the wood had been eaten away by termites for years, the _____ caved in just as Marianne and her family were about to begin eating Thanksgiving dinner.

   1) _____   **2)** _____   **3)** _____

4.   No matter what I do to discourage him, my _____ Ralph sneaks into my room around midnight, jumps on my bed, and sleeps with me until morning.

   1) _____   **2)** _____   **3)** _____

5.   The _____ in front of our house seems to lose more leaves and branches every year.

   1) _____   **2)** _____   **3)** _____

6.   As the temperature dropped to twenty degrees below freezing, the shivering _____ returned to the lodge to warm themselves by the fire.

   1) _____   **2)** _____   **3)** _____

7. Slamming Don's cup of coffee down on the table, _____ snarled, "I hope you're going to have more than a cup of coffee for breakfast."

   1) _____   2) _____   3) _____

8. After Al spilled orange soda on it, Mother's expensive _____ looked more orange than pale gray.

   1) _____   2) _____   3) _____

9. _____, a dish Jeanne had never prepared before, looked very greasy lying there on the white serving platter.

   1) _____   2) _____   3) _____

10. Carefully the _____ inserted a thermometer into my mouth to find out if I had a fever.

    1) _____   2) _____   3) _____

11. When the electricity went off, the humming _____ fell silent.

    1) _____   2) _____   3) _____

12. Ever since Margo was an infant, _____ has always taken her to Jones Beach on Memorial Day.

    1) _____   2) _____   3) _____

Exercise 3-2   Choosing Subjects

INSTRUCTIONS: In each sentence below, you are given a sentence whose subject has not been named. Think about what point is being made about the missing subject. Then write three subjects that might well have performed the action expressed in the sentence. The first one is done for you.

1. Because there are no windows in our office, the _____ often complain about how hot and stuffy the room is.

    1) <u>secretaries</u>   **2)** <u>patients</u>   **3)** <u>customers</u>

2. Quietly the _____ closed his arithmetic book, put his pencil down, and sneaked out the back door.

    1) _____   **2)** _____   **3)** _____

3. The _____ voted against the President's new tax bill at a ratio of two to one.

    1) _____   **2)** _____   **3)** _____

4. The _____ performed our marriage ceremony in Room 484 of Township Hall.

    1) _____   **2)** _____   **3)** _____

5. When its _____ suddenly came apart, the salesman was forced to carry his briefcase under his arm.

    1) _____   **2)** _____   **3)** _____

6. Quietly the _____ whispered to Dee that he wouldn't serve her any more drinks.

    1) _____   **2)** _____   **3)** _____

7. After having sat on a high flame for fifteen minutes, the _____ in the saucepan had entirely boiled away.

    1) _____   **2)** _____   **3)** _____

8. Over the last year or so, the _____ on my bedroom walls
    has peeled so badly that I must redecorate.

    1) _____   2) _____   3) _____

9. While I worked on my math assignment in the family room, the
    _____ blared so loudly that I wasn't able to concentrate on
    my work.

    1) _____   2) _____   3) _____

10. Smiling, the _____ announced that it would cost Ian $600
    to have the engine overhauled.

    1) _____   2) _____   3) _____

11. As he turned to look at a booing fan, the _____ lost control
    of the ball.

    1) _____   2) _____   3) _____

12. The _____ had broken down, so the line of customers
    waiting to pay for their groceries grew longer and longer.

    1) _____   2) _____   3) _____

Exercise 3-3 Revising Subjects

INSTRUCTIONS: When you're revising your rough draft, you may come across a sentence whose words make a very precise point but whose subject—the person, place, or thing the sentence is making a point about—seems general in comparison. Read each of the sentences below carefully enough so that you understand the point being made about the subject of the sentence. Replace the underlined subject with a more specific subject as suggested by the other words in the sentence. Rewrite the entire sentence with your new subject in the blank provided. Feel free to use more than one word as the subject of your sentence. The first one is done for you.

1. The situation with little Mark grew louder as his father placed a forkful of brussel sprouts in front of Mark's mouth.

   Little Mark's screaming grew louder as his
   father placed a forkful of brussel sprouts in
   front of Mark's mouth.

2. After the service the people congratulated the minister for the inspiring sermon he had delivered.

   _____

   _____

   _____

3. All admitted to their biology teacher that they had not yet completed their experiments.

   _____

   _____

   _____

4. <u>The problem with my tooth</u> distracted me from paying attention to the movie.

_____

_____

_____

5. Todd's <u>things</u> seemed to have disappeared from his locker.

_____

_____

_____

6. <u>The guy</u> told me that if my wife didn't like the purple sweater I had just bought her, I should return it within a week.

_____

_____

_____

7. <u>That kid</u> embarrassed me as he shouted, ''Don't swim past the rope!''

_____

_____

_____

8. As the conductor replaced his baton on the podium at the end of the concert, <u>everyone</u> applauded.

_____

_____

_____

Exercise 3-3   Revising Subjects (continued)

9. <u>The people</u> thanked Rhett for having invited them to his fifteenth birthday party.

   _____

   _____

   _____

10. When I arrived for my doctor's appointment, <u>the girl</u> told me that Dr. Jones was a half-hour behind schedule.

   _____

   _____

   _____

11. <u>The things</u> Grandmother put in her stew smelled like decaying garbage.

   _____

   _____

   _____

12. Both striped and polka-dotted, <u>it</u> doesn't complement Mike's glen-plaid suit.

   _____

   _____

   _____

Exercise 3-4   Combining Subjects with Verbs

INSTRUCTIONS: In the items below, you are given a verb as well as words that help complete the meaning of the verb. Supply a subject—someone who might have performed the action—and then complete the sentence by adding words that relate how, when, or where the action might have taken place. The first one is done for you.

1. _____ adjusted her

   glasses _____

   _____.

   Very carefully the math student adjusted her
   glasses since she could not see the equation
   her teacher had just written on the board.

2. _____ cracked two eggs _____

   _____

   _____

   _____.

3. _____ guessed my age _____

   _____

   _____

   _____.

4. _____

   washes the dishes _____

   _____

   _____.

5. _____ has promised her boyfriend _____

_____

_____

_____.

6. _____

_____ mixed wheat germ in with his cereal _____

_____

_____.

7. _____ grabbed the telephone _____

_____

_____

_____.

8. _____

_____ handed Noreen her change _____

_____

_____.

9. _____

_____ poured the milk _____

_____

_____.

10. _____ tied string _____

_____

Exercise 3-4 Combining Subjects with Verbs (continued)

_____

_____.

11. _____ wraps her

sandwich _____

_____

_____.

12. _____ stared at his boss _____

_____

_____.

13. _____ has built a sandcastle _____

_____

_____.

14. _____ fries three strips of bacon _____

_____

_____.

Exercise 3-5   Choosing Verbs

INSTRUCTIONS: In each item below, you are given a sentence whose verb is missing. Therefore, whatever point the writer wants to make about the subject has not been expressed. Read each sentence carefully and supply three verbs that recreate what the subject might have done, given the situation set up in the sentence. The first one is done for you.

1. Because Frank was convicted of deserting his post when the enemy attacked, his commanding officer _____ the medals and buttons from his uniform.

   1) stripped   2) ripped   3) yanked

2. Greedy James _____ his dead mother-in-law's pearl necklace from her jewelry box.

   1) _____   2) _____   3) _____

3. When Charlie saw the elderly Mrs. Odgen carrying a large bag of groceries up her front steps, he _____ to help her.

   1) _____   2) _____   3) _____

4. Every morning at nine o'clock our science instructor, Professor Smith, _____ a cup of black coffee before going to his 9:10 class.

   1) _____   2) _____   3) _____

5. Because Jack and Ernie were laughing and whispering during the movie last night, the six-foot, two-hundred-fifty-pound usher _____ that they leave the theater immediately.

   1) _____   2) _____   3) _____

6. Horrified when she saw the "F" scribbled on her math test, Bea _____ for a solid hour when she got home from school.

   1) _____   2) _____   3) _____

7. This morning while cleaning his room, Michael's mother _____ a stick of dynamite in the top drawer of his bureau, under his T-shirts.

   1) _____   2) _____   3) _____

8. Every New Year's Eve for the past five years Diane has _____ Walter in the main ballroom of the Waldorf Astoria.

   1) _____   2) _____   3) _____

9. After feeling how burned his back was, Nathan _____ that he should have brought along some suntan oil.

   1) _____   2) _____   3) _____

10. Yesterday during his birthday party, Martin _____ constantly; his mother was very embarrassed.

    1) _____   2) _____   3) _____

11. Now that his parents have given him a new car, Randy _____ them at least twice a day.

    1) _____   2) _____   3) _____

12. The music was very loud at the rock concert, but Harvey _____ it anyway.

    1) _____   2) _____   3) _____

13. Little Pam's giggling _____ her father until he realized she was laughing at him.

    1) _____   2) _____   3) _____

14. Even though our teacher Mrs. Calwalader asked her not to, Gloria _____ her foot whenever she wasn't looking.

    1) _____   2) _____   3) _____

Exercise 3-6   Choosing Verbs

INSTRUCTIONS: In the story below the verbs have been omitted so that the reader never knows for sure what point each sentence is making about its subject. Put together the meanings of the words in each sentence, and then write in a verb that fits with the sentence's implied point. The first one is done for you.

    Warren (1) <u>prepared</u> himself for a full Sunday afternoon of watching sports on television, just as he had (2) _____ on previous Sunday afternoons. Even when beautiful women (3) _____ passes at him as he (4) _____ his popcorn and soda at the Quik Chek store, he (5) _____ their advances in order to make sure he (6) _____ on time for his first basketball game. He (7) _____ on the television and (8) _____ out on the couch in the den. After the first basketball game (9) _____ over, he (10) _____ the entire bag of popcorn. Then he (11) _____ for a few minutes. He (12) _____ up when he (13) _____ the boxing match he had (14) _____ to watch being announced. Following this event, he (15) _____ another basketball game, one more boxing match, and an international skiing competition. Finally, he (16) _____ himself away from the television set and (17) _____ some more soda from the kitchen. "Being an athlete sure (18) _____ a lot of preparation," he (19) _____ to himself. "It's a good thing I (20) _____ another week to train for next week's events!"

REVISING VERBS AND COMPLEMENTS

Just as you revise a subject that seems more general than the point you're making about it, so too should you revise a verb and the words that complete its meaning whenever it or they are more general than the rest of the sentence. Here is an example in which the underlined verb and some of its completing words are more general than they need be:

> Because it was about time to close the restaurant, Johnny <u>began to do</u> the grill with soap and water.

The point that the writer wants to make about Johnny only becomes clear when the reader finds out what he's acting upon ("the grill"), how he's doing so ("with soap and water"), and under what circumstances ("because it was about time to close the restaurant").

The words that follow the verb, "began," "to do the grill with soap and water," are called the *complete predicate*. They complete the meaning begun by the verb about the subject. The situation suggested by these words brings to mind a verb like *scrubbed*, a word that can state more exactly what Johnny actually might have done under the circumstances so clearly expressed:

> Because it was about time to close the restaurant, Johnny <u>scrubbed</u> the grill with soap and water.

Here's another example:

> Maria's landlord <u>made a big deal about the party she had the other night.</u>

Again the very general verb "made" leads to equally general completing words, the *complement* of the sentence: "a big deal about the party she had the other night." Once we ask what exactly the landlord did to give us this general impression, we will arrive at a more exact verb which, in turn, will lead to a more informative sentence:

> Maria's landlord <u>warned her that if she ever threw another party like last Saturday night's, he would not renew her lease.</u>

Another example,

> Mr. Howard <u>gave Mrs. Howard a hand</u> as she repaired the garage roof.

becomes a better sentence with revision:

Mr. Howard <u>handed Mrs. Howard the shingles and nails</u> as she repaired the garage roof.

Remember: in some of the sentences in the following exercises you may only need to come up with one word to make their points clearer. In others you may have to think up a verb plus some completing words in order to make their points clearer. As long as all your sentence parts fit together when you read them, and as long as they make the point of your sentences clearer, you can conclude that you have revised them successfully. Read them aloud to a friend to make sure.

Exercise 3-7   Revising Weak Verbs

INSTRUCTIONS: In each sentence below replace the underlined, general verbs and complements with more meaningful ones. Write your revised verbs and complements in the space provided. The first one is done for you.

1.   Although she had started to write it weeks earlier, Joan finally <u>did her assignment</u> Sunday night, the night before it was due.

   <u>finished writing her history term paper.</u>

2.   When the family had seated themselves at the table, Father <u>proceeded to do the passing of the food</u>.

   _____

   _____

3.   Since Johnny seldom wears warm socks in the fall and winter, he usually <u>has a lot of health problems</u>.

   _____

   _____

4.   When the coach shouts, "Get movin', Smith!" every time I need to catch my breath, I <u>get mad</u>.

   _____

   _____

5.   Arriving home about two hours after his curfew, Max <u>went in</u>.

   _____

   _____

6. While carrying two plates of spaghetti as well as three bowls of chili above the heads of the crowd of diners, the waiter <u>had some bad luck</u>.

_____

_____

7. While Paul stood on the top step of the shaky ladder changing a light bulb, <u>I decided to help</u>.

_____

_____

8. Ida's husband Percy always <u>gives her a hard time</u> when she comes home late on her bowling night.

_____

_____

9. Sad to say, Ralph <u>gets crazy</u> whenever he loses money playing poker.

_____

_____

10. Shocked when he saw the engagement ring on Fran's finger, her boyfriend Claude <u>started to have ideas about how faithful she was</u>.

_____

_____

Exercise 3-8 Revising Weak Verbs

INSTRUCTIONS: In each sentence below, replace the underlined, general verbs and complements with more meaningful ones. Write your revised verbs and complements in the space provided. The first one is done for you.

1. Several times I <u>tried,</u> but the engine still wouldn't start.

   <u>turned the key in the ignition,</u>

2. As Charlie hurried nervously down a dangerous unlighted street very late at night, a tall, thin man waving a switchblade <u>came up</u>.

   _____

   _____

3. Just as her friends kissed her and shouted "Happy Birthday!" Marianne <u>began to be excited</u>.

   _____

   _____

4. So that she arrives at her job as a security guard precisely at midnight, Sarah <u>makes sure to get herself up</u>.

   _____

   _____

5. Every day from three to six Murray <u>kept on doing his basketball playing nearby</u> in order to win a place on his high school team.

   _____

   _____

6. My cousin Frank, who ate lunch at our house, <u>made a mess of the kitchen</u>.

   _____

   _____

7. Exhausted from having worked twelve hours straight waxing floors at J. C. Penney's, Arthur <u>left</u>.

   _____

   _____

8. All Sunday afternoon Tim <u>got himself together</u> for the week because the previous week his boss had complained that his clothes always looked wrinkled.

   _____

   _____

9. Although he was five minutes late arriving at the station, George <u>made it</u>.

   _____

   _____

10. Rich <u>had trust in his friend Bob as far as his car was concerned</u>.

    _____

    _____

11. The heavy woolen jacket Sally wore <u>got in her way</u>.

    _____

    _____

Exercise 3-9 Revising Weak Verbs

INSTRUCTIONS: In each sentence below, replace the underlined, general verbs and complements with more meaningful ones. Write your revised verbs and complements in the space provided. The first one is done for you.

1. Max gave some assistance to the elderly woman boarding the bus.

   supported the arm of

2. At exactly the stroke of noon, the bride and groom got started as the organist played "The Wedding March."

3. My history professor, Mr. Edwards, gave me some leads on a term paper.

4. Edna was very confused by the form the clerk had given her at the Motor Vehicle office; she took a lot of time with it.

5. Mimi acted up when the waiter at the Seafood Shanty didn't seem to notice her new dress.

6. After she had eaten her supper, Marnie started to go to do her English essay.

7. The sales clerk in Bamberger's men's department <u>gave me a hard time</u> when I returned my new shirt with a hole in it.

_____

_____

8. The little boy <u>fussed</u> when his mother told him it was time to leave the beach.

_____

_____

9. Every morning at breakfast Jack <u>says nice things to his new bride Laura</u>.

_____

_____

10. Laura, who is often irritable in the morning, usually <u>says something obnoxious</u>.

_____

_____

11. After it was fertilized and watered, the apple tree <u>changed</u>.

_____

_____

12. Expert baker that she is, Lena <u>went all out for her husband's birthday cake</u>.

_____

_____

Exercise 3-10   Combining Verbs with Subjects

INSTRUCTIONS: In the following items, you are given a subject with adjectives that help identify the subject more precisely. Taking your cues from the situation suggested by each subject and its adjective modifiers, complete the sentence by adding a verb or complete predicate to describe how, when, and where the subject acted and, if called for, on what or whom it acted. The first one is done for you.

1. The sputtering car engine <u>stalled in the middle lane</u>

    <u>of the George Washington Bridge during the</u>

    <u>evening rush hour.</u>

2. The surprised teacher _____

    _____

    _____

    _____.

3. The woman who works as a waitress at the Mayflower Cafe _____

    _____

    _____

    _____.

4. Surprised by the party his friend Todd was giving him, Wendall __

    _____

    _____

    _____.

5. Knowing he was doing the wrong thing, my brother Mark _____

    _____

_____

_____.

6. The mysterious woman wearing the black dress _____

_____

_____

_____.

7. Pleased that he had gotten home from work early, Ernie's wife _____

_____

_____

_____.

8. Shouting at the top of his lungs, the rock singer _____

_____

_____

_____.

9. My supervisor at work, who is usually in a bad mood, _____

_____

_____

_____.

10. The engine of Carla's 1955 Ford _____

_____

_____

_____.

Exercise 3-10 Combining Verbs with Subjects (continued)

11. My Aunt Clarissa, whom I hadn't heard from in fifteen years, _____

_____

_____

_____.

12. The grinning used-car salesman _____

_____

_____

_____.

13. Stretching out on her bed after a hard day's work, Lisa _____

_____

_____

_____.

14. Suddenly standing up, the loan officer at the bank _____

_____

_____

_____.

STRENGTHENING VERBS WITH ADVERBS

Choosing a subject to talk about is like directing a character to come onto an empty stage. Combining a verb with that subject is like directing the character to act in a certain way so that the play can get under way. Hence, the verb of the sentence is what moves the subject in order to create the sentence's idea, for example:

The soprano sang. . . .

English sentence structures allow you to reinforce the meaning of the verb with words called *adverbs*. They reinforce the meaning of the verb by telling the reader when the subject did what you said it did, where it did so, and how it did so. For example:

The soprano sang <u>as if the music had been written just for her</u>. (how)

The soprano sang <u>on stage</u>. (where)

The soprano sang <u>at the end of the second act</u>. (when)

Telling how, when, or where the action of the sentence takes place allows your reader to imagine the action you are recreating more clearly.

Adverbs and word groups that act like adverbs come in three forms: one-word adverbs, adverb phrases, and adverb clauses:

The soprano sang <u>beautifully</u>. (one word)

The soprano sang <u>on stage</u>. (phrase)

The soprano sang <u>as if the music had been written just for her</u>. (clause)

ONE-WORD ADVERBS

Sometimes all you need to make clear how, when, or where the action of a sentence has taken place is one word:

The man who had shot himself in the foot walked <u>haltingly</u>. (how)

The senator <u>often</u> made excuses for not keeping her appointments. (when)

Sid jumped <u>up</u> from his seat and shouted "Bingo!" (where)

ADVERB PHRASES

You can also use groups of words that act like adverbs. A common type of this kind of adverb is the prepositional phrase adverb. It combines a preposition with a noun, as in "on the carpet," "at eight o'clock," or "throughout the day." These phrases, like one-word adverbs, tell you when, where, or how the action of the sentence has taken place. For example:

Marjorie ate her meat loaf <u>with a glass of milk</u>. (how)

Lightning struck the barn <u>at midnight</u>. (when)

The referree placed the football <u>on the twenty yard line</u>. (where)

Prepositions usually indicate either time or place. Some commonly used prepositions include the following:

on	to	off	beneath
in	by	during	between
at	from	around	out of
below	onto	against	into
under	above	along	on top of
among	after	near	inside of
across	up	beside	until

ADVERB CLAUSES

The other type of adverb that combines words in groups is the *adverb clause*. It is the most complex form for an adverb to take. It contains a subject and a complete predicate, just like a sentence, but it cannot stand by itself. It always begins with a connecting word called an *adverbial conjunction* (or subordinate conjunction). Some of the most commonly used connecting words include:

when	until	if	as long as
so that	since	while	as if
although	as	before	in order that
unless	after	as soon as	

An adverbial conjunction joins the subject and complete predicate that follow it to the main verb of the sentence so that the entire clause can give the reader information about how, when, or where the action of the sentence took place, for instance:

As soon as Tess removed the cotter pin, the wheel of her little red wagon fell off.

The subject and complete predicate of the adverb clause ("Tess removed the cotter pin") make the action more imaginable since we are told *when* the wheel fell off. Notice also that when the adverb clause falls first in the sentence it is followed by a comma at the end of the introductory clause. This is one of the major uses of the comma in English—setting the stage for the all-important main subject and verb.

REVISING ADVERBS

Now that you are more familiar with the different kinds of adverbs, you can use them in revising your own writing to give your ideas more meaning. For instance, in the following sentence, the writer puts together a fairly specific subject, verb, and some words to complete the meaning of the predicate. Notice though that the adverb phrase used to complete the meaning of the predicate does not tell us very much about how the action of the sentence took place:

The cafeteria worker had never talked to me <u>so weird before</u>.

As readers we understand that the writer is in a cafeteria being addressed *in some way* by a cafeteria worker. Unless this is a topic sentence meant to introduce a paragraph-length explanation of the way the worker addressed the writer, the writer is probably better off stating *how* the worker addressed her. She should try to give her reader a way of imagining or experiencing what manner of address the worker used:

The cafeteria worker had never talked to me <u>in such a friendly way before</u>.

The cafeteria worker had never talked to me so <u>rudely</u> before.

The cafeteria worker had never before talked to me <u>as if I were a four-year-old who knew nothing about proper nutrition</u>.

If you find yourself using general adverbs where more specific ones could be provided, ask yourself for details of how, when, or where the action of the sentence took place, and then replace the more general forms with more detailed and descriptive adverbs.

_____

Exercise 3-11   One-word Adverbs

INSTRUCTIONS: In the sentences that follow, think up two *one-word* adverbs that explain how, when, or where the action of the sentence has taken place and write them in the spaces provided. The first one is done for you.

1. The audience applauded _____ when the rock star returned to the stage to play another song.

    1) <u>wildly</u>   2) <u>enthusiastically</u>

2. The student clenched his fist _____ as his English instructor read his essay.

    1) _____   2) _____

3. _____ Mary does not care for spaghetti as much as she used to.

    1) _____   2) _____

4. The generous hostess filled her guests' glasses _____.

    1) _____   2) _____

5. _____ Arthur ran out of the diner to put a dime in the parking meter.

    1) _____   2) _____

6. _____ Rick ignored his neighbors' demands to lower the volume on his stereo.

    1) _____   2) _____

7. The new mother _____ rocked her infant to sleep.

    1) _____   2) _____

8. I _____ passed my calculus test last week.

    1) _____   2) _____

9. Aretha _____ retold her story to the police officer who had not witnessed her accident.

    1) _____   2) _____

10. _____ the man who had not eaten for several days gobbled the sirloin steak.

    1) _____   2) _____

11. _____ the teacher announced that our history quiz was rescheduled for next week.

    1) _____   2) _____

Exercise 3-12   Prepositional Adverb Phrases

INSTRUCTIONS: In the sentences below, imagine the situation being related, and then write two prepositional phrases to make clear how, when, or where the action of the sentence takes place. The following prepositions may be useful, but use whatever prepositions seem to follow naturally from the context of the sentence:

on	to	off	beneath
in	by	during	between
at	from	around	out of
below	onto	against	into
under	above	along	on top of
among	after	near	inside of
across	up	beside	until

The first one is done for you.

1.   Rod placed his top hat _____ as he left to pick up his date for the New Year's Eve formal.

   1) <u>on the back</u>   **2)** <u>just above his eyebrows</u>

   <u>of his head</u>

2.   Father placed the crystal bowl of apples, grapes, and bananas _____.

   1) _____   **2)** _____

3.   _____ John's clock-radio blared, waking him out of a long sleep.

   1) _____   **2)** _____

4.   Frank hid his dirty underwear _____ so that his room would look neat.

   1) _____   **2)** _____

5. The patrol officer escorted the kindergartner safely _____.

   1) _____   **2)** _____

6. The Marshalls have lived _____ for the past twenty-five years.

   1) _____   **2)** _____

7. The frightened toddler tottered cautiously _____.

   1) _____   **2)** _____

8. Jake lifted the pitcher of beer _____ so that none of the partiers would disturb it.

   1) _____   **2)** _____

9. Marie hoped to finish cleaning her bedroom _____ so that she could then go to the beach.

   1) _____   **2)** _____

10. While we were vacationing in the Rockies, Alice took a picture of Tina and me _____.

    1) _____   **2)** _____

11. Anxiously, Father climbed _____ to rescue our cat Felix.

    1) _____   **2)** _____

12. Father angrily demanded that I take my shoes _____.

    1) _____   **2)** _____

_____

Exercise 3-13   Adverb Clauses

INSTRUCTIONS: Read each sentence below carefully, and develop its meaning further by adding an adverb clause to relate how, when, or where the action of the sentence takes place. The following adverbial conjunctions may be useful, but use any others that seem to flow naturally from the context of the sentence:

when	until	if	as long as
so that	since	while	as if
although	as	before	in order that
unless	after	as soon as	

If the sentence you write *begins* with a clause, make sure to put a comma at the end of the adverb clause. The first one is done for you.

1.   Yawning, the exhausted postal clerk weighed still another

   Christmas package <u>as she waited for the long line</u>

   <u>of Christmas–eve customers to come to an end.</u>

2.   The needle scratched the record _____

   _____

   _____.

3.   Last week at Macy's I spent three hundred dollars on new clothes

   _____

   _____.

4.   _____

   _____

   Hermoine, my late sister-in-law, did not remember me in her will.

5.   _____

   _____

Michael won't ever speak to his twin brother Marty ever again.

6. _____

_____

Cathy has a chance to pass Accounting 101.

7. _____

_____

I'll feed my sister's dog Fido every evening at seven o'clock.

8. _____

_____

Grandpa turned on more lights in the living room.

9. Matthew's Uncle Dan shed a few tears of joy _____

_____

_____.

10. _____

_____

Robert phoned his boss to tell him that he wouldn't be coming to work anymore.

11. Iris apologized to the woman sitting in front of her at the movies

_____

_____.

Exercise 3-14   Adverb Clauses

INSTRUCTIONS: In this exercise you are given the adverb clause that tells you when, how, or under what circumstances the action of the sentence takes place. Complete each sentence by adding a specific and complete subject and predicate to tell exactly what that action is and write the sentence in the space provided. Remember to place a comma at the end of an introductory adverb clause. The first one is done for you.

1. just as my history professor shouted, "Time's up!"

    I wrote the last word for my final essay just as my history professor shouted, "Time's up!"

2. until he practiced playing the piano for an hour

    _____

    _____

    _____.

3. although Rita usually listens to classical music when she gets up in the morning

    _____

    _____

    _____.

4. while my husband barbecued the hot dogs

    _____

    _____

    _____.

5. whenever her boss watches her as she stocks the shelves

    _____

_____

_____ .

6. after she hammered the nail into the curtain fixture

_____

_____

_____ .

7. if the 'e' on my typewriter continues to stick

_____

_____

_____ .

8. until the bus company raises its rates

_____

_____

_____ .

9. as soon as the disc jockey announced the name of the record he was going to play

_____

_____

_____ .

10. so that Peter would be able to pay for the expensive tickets to the rock concert

_____

_____

_____ .

Exercise 3-14   Adverb Clauses (continued)

11.   before Father hid his fifth of twelve-year-old scotch behind his Barcalounger

_____

_____

_____.

12.   as I was driving to school this morning

_____

_____

_____.

NAME _____

Exercise 3-15   Choosing Adverbs

INSTRUCTIONS: In the story below, adverb forms have been omitted or left incomplete. Therefore, it's very difficult to imagine when, where, or how the action of the story takes place. Read through the story completely to get an idea of what kind of action is being related. Then supply whatever words you think will supply the story's missing hows, whens, and wheres. The first one is done for you.

My friend Jake threw himself a twenty-first birthday party last Saturday night. I didn't have a very good time.

When I (1) <u>walked through Jake's front door</u>, I heard the throbbing sounds of a rock and roll band. The lead guitarist played as

if (2) _____.

The drummer pounded the drums (3) _____ly

while the hundred partiers (4) _____

_____.

Then, I noticed a bar had been set up next to (5) _____,

behind the plaid sofa. Jake provided gin, scotch, and whiskey; in fact, he

offered his guests as much liquor as they (6) _____

_____. (7) _____, I grabbed

myself a beer and walked (8) _____ and (9) _____,

looking for somebody that I knew to (10) _____.

Sitting on (11) _____ in the den, Jennifer, whom

I had dated for (12) _____, smiled (13) _____

_____ly at (14) _____

and asked me to sit down next to (15) _____. I,

of course, was happy that she had spoken to me, although (16) _____

_____.

After we (17) _____, we chatted for (18) _____

_____ about old times. I reminded her how we used to go

hiking every (19) _____, especially when (20) _____

_____. (21) _____ly, she said

how much she had missed me and that she wanted to marry me if

(22) _____. This remark was much more frightening than if

(23) _____. (24) _____ly, I ex-

cused myself and said that I had to go (25) _____ to

(26) _____ and ten children.

Exercise 3-16　Revising Adverbs

INSTRUCTIONS: Read the sentences below carefully to make sure you follow what point is being related. Then replace the underlined general adverb form with one that states more directly how, when, or where the action of the sentence takes place. Let your adverbs flow naturally from the situation set up in the sentence. You may have to think up a one-word adverb, an adverb phrase, or an adverb clause. Write your adverb forms in the space provided. The first one is done for you.

1. Our family spends two weeks in August <u>there</u>.

   <u>at a rented cottage on the beach</u>

2. My Aunt Bertha <u>always</u> makes fresh lemonade.

   _____

3. Whenever I ask my brother for some money, he usually screams <u>that way</u>.

   _____

4. Peter lent his umbrella to his sister Rhea <u>then</u>.

   _____

5. When Tim asked Martha to marry him, she kissed him <u>everywhere</u>.

   _____

6. <u>Next</u> the waiter poured the coffee.

   _____

7. Every summer my family travels <u>far away</u> on our vacation.

   _____

8. <u>By doing that</u> three-year-old Jimmy hoped he could convince Santa Claus to bring him a bicycle for Christmas.

   _____

9. When shopping, Marie eats her lunch <u>in that place</u>.

_____

10. My father works two jobs <u>in order to do that</u>.

_____

11. <u>Since that was the case</u>, the baseball coach changed his mind about cutting Frank from the team.

_____

12. <u>After that happened</u>, the car came to a sudden halt.

_____

13. Winnie agreed to ride the roller coaster <u>only under those circumstances</u>.

_____

14. <u>For that reason</u> Sam never drinks coffee at breakfast.

_____

15. Whenever he goes out on Saturday night, Rick always dresses <u>that way</u>.

_____

16. I walk in my sleep every night <u>at that time</u>.

_____

17. <u>Since that was the way things were</u>, Tom decided not to panel his bedroom.

_____

18. <u>Having done that</u>, the mail carrier frightened away the barking bull dog.

_____

STRENGTHENING NOUNS WITH ADJECTIVES

Sometimes when you use a noun to name a person, place, or thing, your reader may have trouble imagining it because you are not being as specific as possible. For example:

chair
woman
teacup

English sentence structures allow you to reinforce nouns with words called *adjectives* that describe the nouns more specifically. For instance,

<u>The oak rocking</u> chair. . . .
<u>The young</u> woman <u>wearing the yellow raincoat</u>. . . .
<u>The</u> teacup <u>that was chipped around the edge.</u>

In this way your reader can understand your sentence more fully, visualizing the item or person you refer to.

Adjectives answer reader-questions like:

<u>Which</u> chair are you referring to?
<u>What kind</u> of woman do you mean?
<u>Which one</u> of the teacups are you making a point about?

When rereading your rough drafts, should you come upon a person, place, or thing that you can't quite place, ask yourself which person, place, or thing you're referring to. Then supply the word or words that will make clear which noun you are talking about by describing it more specifically. Describe how it looked, felt, sounded, tasted, or smelled.

ONE-WORD ADJECTIVES

The simplest form of adjective is a one-word adjective, such as:

<u>shouting</u> neighbors
<u>mahogany</u> table
<u>double</u> cheeseburger

The underlined words are adjectives in that they describe for readers which neighbors, table, or cheeseburger you mean to say something about. One-word adjectives can also be added together in a chain to be even more descriptive about a noun:

The shouting neighbors. . . .
Our new mahogany table. . . .
An enormous double cheeseburger. . . .
My old 1967 red and black convertible Mustang. . . .

ADJECTIVE PHRASES

Just as prepositional phrases can answer questions about how, when, or where something has happened, they can also answer questions like which one or what kind of person, place, or thing you are referring to. Prepositional phrases can, in other words, also do the work of adjectives. For example, in this sentence

The usher escorted my wife and me to our seats.

you could identify more completely the usher who escorted you and your wife by recalling what the usher looked like:

The usher in the red velvet jacket. . . .

The usher with bushy eyebrows. . . .

Now your readers can visualize the person much better. Some common prepositions include the following:

with	except	below	within
behind	on	by	from
under	next to	into	through
in front of	to	inside	toward
out	above	over	like
in	around	up	across
at	beside	off	between
of			

ADJECTIVE CLAUSES

The most complex form of adjective that is used in English is the *adjective clause.* Just like the adverb clause, it is called a clause because it contains a subject and a complete predicate. A sentence like

The cat meowed.

can be turned into an adjective clause by using "meowed" to identify which cat you mean:

The cat <u>that meowed on the back porch</u> hadn't yet eaten her supper.

Notice how the word "that" stands for the cat you're making a point about. Words that stand for nouns are called *pronouns*. In addition to *that*, the words *who* and *which* are pronouns that will introduce adjective clauses, such as:

A man <u>who lives in my neighborhood</u> has never heard of Ronald Reagan.

My penmanship, <u>which can hardly be deciphered</u>, is a mark of my artistic genius.

Adjective clauses use *who* when referring to a person and *that* or *which* when referring to a thing. Notice also that the adjective clause "which can hardly be deciphered" interrupts the point you are making and that a comma is placed before and after the interruption.

REVISING ADJECTIVES

Often beginning writers are more general in choosing words and word combinations than they should be. A writer might describe her best friend as being "nice," when subsequent sentences clearly indicate that what she really has in mind is that she is "polite" or "generous."

Or, a writer might say that the shirt he wore to Friday night's party was "boring," when all he means is that the shirt was "out of style." In both instances, revising the general adjectives by replacing them with more telling ones allows readers to understand and visualize more easily what the writer is making a point about.

So the moral is clear. When revising your rough drafts, look for words that don't carry as much meaning or description as they might, often the result of using an adjective that is not specific enough. Such general adjectives are often produced when a writer depends too much on verbs that are "at rest" instead of "in action." For instance, in this sentence "Jeff," the subject, is not performing any action. The verb "was" simply acts like an equal sign to connect "Jeff" with "nice":

Jeff <u>was nice</u> to his brother Charles while Charles was recovering from chicken pox.

If this sentence is to be the topic sentence of a paragraph detailing Jeff's many acts of sympathy toward his suffering brother, the sentence would set up the paragraph much better if it read:

Jeff <u>was most sympathetic toward</u> his brother Charles while Charles was recovering from chicken pox.

If, on the other hand, this sentence is meant to act out a larger point about Jeff—that he is thoughtful or kind, for example—then the writer would be better off replacing the inactive verb and adjective ("was nice") with a more active verb and complement:

Jeff **bought a dozen comic books** for his brother Charles while Charles was recovering from chicken pox.

Also revise adjectives that simply suggest your point of view in a general way, as in these sentences:

My new tie is a **terrific** color of green.

Georgina spent **too much** time talking on the phone last night.

These are passable as opening sentences of paragraphs meant to explain them in more detail. However, make sure that you become more descriptive than this in your explanations. Instead of using propagandistic adjectives like "terrific" or "too much," supply your readers with what you observed, and let them draw their own conclusions. Or better, let them see where *your* conclusions come from:

My new tie is **emerald** green.

Georgina spent **an hour and a half** talking on the phone last night. She never completed her homework assignment.

Exercise 3-17   One-word Adjectives

INSTRUCTIONS: In the items below, read each sentence and think of two one-word adjectives that, as far as possible, allow you to see, hear, taste, smell, or touch the person, place, or thing the sentence is making a point about. The first one is done for you.

1. The _____ dog lazily rolled over and went back to sleep.

    1) mangy   2) yawning

2. While wrestling with his younger brother in the living room, Jack knocked over the _____ vase.

    1) _____   2) _____

3. The barber said, "Next!" so I lowered myself into the _____ chair.

    1) _____   2) _____

4. Father emptied the pitcher of _____ milk into little Sarah's glass.

    1) _____   2) _____

5. The quarterback fumbled the _____ football after the center hiked it to him.

    1) _____   2) _____

6. Martin threaded the needle before sewing the _____ buttons onto his red-and-blue flannel shirt.

    1) _____   2) _____

7. Shana thinned the _____ paint by pouring in some turpentine.

    1) _____   2) _____

8. The dinner guest confided to his hostess that the ＿＿＿＿＿＿ peas she offered him nauseated him.

    1) ＿＿＿＿＿＿＿＿＿＿　　　　2) ＿＿＿＿＿＿＿＿＿＿

9. Father hid Martha's Easter basket behind the ＿＿＿＿＿＿ chair.

    1) ＿＿＿＿＿＿＿＿＿＿　　　　2) ＿＿＿＿＿＿＿＿＿＿

10. The bat living in the ＿＿＿＿＿＿ attic searched for a window when I turned on the light.

    1) ＿＿＿＿＿＿＿＿＿＿　　　　2) ＿＿＿＿＿＿＿＿＿＿

11. Roger grabbed the ＿＿＿＿＿＿ book out of Richard's hand so that he could study for Friday's test.

    1) ＿＿＿＿＿＿＿＿＿＿　　　　2) ＿＿＿＿＿＿＿＿＿＿

Exercise 3-18   Adjective Phrases

INSTRUCTIONS: Supply prepositional phrases in the sentences below so that, as far as possible, they allow you to visualize the person, place, or thing you're making a point about. Here is a list of common prepositions you can use, but you should try to use whatever ones come to mind as you read each sentence:

with	except	below	within
behind	on	by	from
under	next to	into	through
in front of	to	inside	toward
out	above	over	like
in	around	up	across
at	beside	off	between
of			

The first one is done for you.

1. The sidewalk _____ always seems to be littered with dirty paper plates, cups, and candy wrappers.

    1) <u>in front of McDonald's</u>   **2)** <u>through the park</u>

2. A summer _____ is not my idea of a pleasant vacation.

    1) _____   **2)** _____

3. My best friend Ruth lives in the house _____.

    1) _____   **2)** _____

4. The dishes _____ all need to be washed.

    1) _____   **2)** _____

5. June handed her ticket to the man _____.

    1) _____   **2)** _____

6. The bottle of beer _____ left an indelible stain.

    1) _____   **2)** _____

7. The chandelier _____ looks as if it's going to fall to the floor.

    1) _____   **2)** _____

8. One pink carnation _____ was brown around the edges.

    1) _____   **2)** _____

9. Lisa passed a note to the student _____.

    1) _____   **2)** _____

10. The elderly man _____ was not able to speak English.

    1) _____   **2)** _____

NAME _____

Exercise 3-19 Adjective Clauses

INSTRUCTIONS: In each sentence below add an adjective clause to
help identify the person, place, or thing named. Use "who" when
referring to a person and "that" or "which" when referring to a thing.
  Use "which" when your clause interrupts the point you're making,
and place a comma before and after the interruption. The first one is
done for you.

1. The manager ran out of the dugout to argue with the umpire _____

    who had called the runner out at home plate.

2. Mona gulped down a tall glass of ice tea _____

    _____

    _____.

3. Jed carefully erased the marks _____

    _____

    _____.

4. The peaches _____

    _____

    _____

    are quite hard.

5. The police officer took the hand of the little boy _____

    _____

    _____.

6. The secretary _____

_____

_____

then asked me to take a seat.

7. The barbells _____

_____

_____ rolled

down the stairs and crushed my shoes.

8. I carefully fertilized the Azalea bush _____

_____

_____.

9. The seagull _____

_____

_____ wasn't

able to fly.

10. The woman _____

_____

_____

told me I wasn't eligible for unemployment benefits.

Exercise 3-20   Choosing Adjectives

INSTRUCTIONS: In the story below, adjective forms have been omitted or left incomplete. Therefore, it's difficult for a reader to visualize, hear, smell, taste, or touch the people, places, and things that are part of the action of the story. Read through the story completely. Then go back and fill in the blanks with whatever words seem necessary to complete the descriptions of the nouns used in the story. The first one is done for you.

A NEEDED CHANGE

For (1) <u>five</u> months, I wanted to change my job because I found it

very (2) _____. You see, I washed (3) _____ dishes for

a living at a (4) _____ diner.

One reason I wanted to quit was that the work was truly (5) _____

_____. Joe, the guy who (6) _____ refused to wash

the really (7) _____ ones, so, since I was new on the job, I had

to wash them. One time a (8) _____ egg had been stuck on a

(9) _____ plate all day before I had the "opportunity" to

wash it. No matter how many times I dunked the (10) _____ dish

into the (11) _____ water, nothing happened. It was as

if the egg would not allow itself to be dissolved.

Meanwhile the (12) _____ floor, which customers

always (13) _____, was covered with a (14) _____,

(15) _____ film of (16) _____ grease and

(17) _____ water.

And my boss was (18) _____. Picture a guy wearing (19) _____, who never (20) _____ _____. You've never met anybody like him. He also had a (21) _____ _____ temper. The sparkle in (22) _____ _____ and the smile on (23) _____ would disappear fast if he discovered I had made the (24) _____ est mistake.

I finally asked myself, "Why am I putting up with this?" I told him he was the (25) _____est character I had ever come across and that he could have his (26) _____ job back.

Now I'm (27) _____-years-old and live off my (28) _____ parents.

Exercise 3-21   Revising Adjectives

INSTRUCTIONS: In the sentences below, revise the underlined word with words that make the meaning of the sentence clearer. Write your revision in the space provided. In some sentences you will have to replace an adjective while in other sentences you will have to replace inactive verbs and adjectives with more active verbs and words to fill out the verb's meaning. The first one is done for you.

1. Chris <u>did a good job on</u> her history term paper.

   earned an A
   _____

2. Lying out on the table all night, the cheddar cheese <u>went bad</u>.

   _____

3. Last week, Mrs. Ruiz gave us a math test <u>that was hard</u>.

   _____

4. At the beach last weekend, Virginia met a surfer <u>with a fantastic body</u>.

   _____

5. Miles Davis <u>is a great jazz musician</u>.

   _____

6. The shirt that Max wore to school today <u>looked weird</u>.

   _____

7. Maria <u>took a lot of time</u> completing her physiology test.

   _____

8. The appreciative audience, <u>who gave them a big applause</u>, encouraged the rock band to play another song.

   _____

9. Last night <u>this guy</u> came into the bar, bragging about how muscular he was.

_____

10. <u>These lights</u> never seem to work when I plug them in.

_____

11. Christine would never have chosen <u>that carpet</u> if she had been at the store with Hank when he bought it.

_____

12. <u>Those customers</u> annoyed Edwin.

_____

13. The father <u>with the happy expression</u> watched as his firstborn graduated from high school.

_____

14. The day <u>that was very sad</u> arrived, so Cathy began to cry.

_____

15. The Whalens, <u>who have a big family</u>, won last month's New Jersey Million Dollar Lottery.

_____

_____

Exercise 3-22　Revising Adjectives

INSTRUCTIONS: In the sentences below, revise the underlined word with words that make the meaning of the sentence clearer. Write your revision in the space provided. In some sentences you will have to replace an adjective while in other sentences you will have to replace inactive verbs and adjectives with more active verbs and words to fill out the verb's meaning. The first one is done for you.

1. The waiter at Friendly's Ice Cream squirted <u>too much whipped cream</u> on my chocolate sundae.

   so much whipped cream on my chocolate sundae

   that it dripped down the sides of the

   container.

2. The mother <u>was glad</u> when her sixty-year-old son told her he had finally decided to marry.

   _____

3. Marvin <u>was mad</u> when he opened the envelope to discover that Sears would give him no further credit.

   _____

4. <u>Some basketballs</u> were stolen from the school gym this morning.

   _____

5. The movie I saw last night, *Hermione and Henry Go to Fort Lauderdale on Their Spring Break*, <u>was just boring</u>.

   _____

6. The lifeguard, <u>who had been mean to Anne</u>, later apologized.

   _____

7. The spaghetti sauce Lorenzo concocted <u>was terrible</u>.

_____

8. The student sitting behind Dee in music class <u>was obnoxious</u>.

_____

9. Before dinner the hostess offered her guests <u>different treats</u>.

_____

10. The way Tommy cut the lawn <u>was ridiculous</u>.

_____

11. After having worked on her sociology term paper all night, Geraldine realized that her room <u>was an awful mess</u>.

_____

12. My best friend Rob <u>had a funny look on his face</u> when I asked him if I could date his fiancée.

_____

13. When you save <u>a certain number of cereal boxtops</u>, you will receive another box free.

_____

14. "Please excuse Johnny's absence from school yesterday; he <u>was sick</u>."

_____

MORE TOPICS FOR WRITING AND REVISING

The following topics are derived from openings of some very fine short stories by authors who have enriched the language you use every day in your socializing, thinking, and communicating. Read each passage to yourself. Then read it aloud as dramatically as possible. Try to hear and reproduce the tone you think the words suggest. When you come across a word or expression you don't understand, try to narrow its meaning by thinking what kinds of meanings would make sense at that point in the sentence and paragraph. Discuss possibilities with your fellow students, and then think about the meanings offered in the dictionary.

To get yourself to think ever more closely about how the author may have written and revised the opening of his or her story, work through the exercises that follow it. The first question asks you to respond to the opening as a whole. How do the general remarks and details work together to give you a unified view of a situation or character? The second allows you to think about the author's words even more deeply by directing you to supply further complementary details: You become co-author. Third, you are asked to continue the story in whatever way you believe makes sense, given how the story begins. Read your passage and continuation of it together and decide if you've begun to make the story your own.

Finally, you are asked to make the jump to your own experience by writing and revising an explanation of a topic drawn from the situation set up in the opening of the story. In writing and revising your composition, your job is *not* to write about the opening of the story, but to write about an incident in your own life that the story opening suggests.

In revising your composition, apply the strategies of question and answer by reading your own rough draft and having your partner read it. This is the kind of assignment that will allow you to see, if you don't already, the intimate connection between reading and writing and how they feed off one another.

One last point. To see how the author developed and concluded his or her story, go to your library and look up a copy of the story. You may be surprised.

Exercise 3-23 Writing Topics

INSTRUCTIONS: Read the passage below, answer the questions that
follow, and write and revise a composition on the given topic.

INSECURITY

Opening of John Cheever's "The Country Husband" (taken from John
Cheever, *The Housebreaker of Shady Hill*, published by Harper & Row,
1958).

To begin at the beginning, the airplane from Minneapolis in which Francis Weed was traveling East ran into heavy weather. [1]The sky had been a
hazy blue with the clouds below the plane lying so close together that
nothing could be seen of the earth. Then mist began to form outside the
windows, and they flew into a white cloud of such density that it reflected
the exhaust fires. [2]The color of the cloud darkened to gray, and the plane
began to rock. Francis had been in heavy weather before, but he had never
been shaken up so much. [3]The man in the seat beside him pulled a flask out
of his pocket and took a drink. Francis smiled at his neighbor, but the man
looked away; he wasn't sharing his painkiller with anyone. The plane began
to drop and flounder wildly. A child was crying. [4]The air in the cabin was
overheated and stale, and Francis' left foot went to sleep. He read a little
from a paper book that he had bought at the airport, but the violence of the
storm divided his attention. It was black outside the ports. [5]The exhaust
fires blazed and shed sparks in the dark, and, inside, the shaded lights, the
stuffiness, and the window curtains gave the cabin an atmosphere of mis-
placed domesticity. Then the lights flickered and went out. . . .

1. Changes in our environment affect the way we feel and think.
    Notice how the details of this opening passage work together to
    describe the main character's changing environment. Describe in
    two or three sentences what kind of environment is recreated here.

_____

_____

_____

_____

2. The numbers 1 to 5 in the excerpt you have just read correspond to the directions below. Following these directions, compose sentences that develop the story's opening even further. Read your newly revised passage aloud to hear if it helps your reader imagine this scene a little differently. The first one is done for you.

   1) Relate what Francis had been doing before the weather got "heavy."

      Francis had been staring out the window,

      trying to imagine the kind of terrain that

      lay below the thick blanket of clouds.

   2) Describe what the rocking of the plane felt like.

      _____

      _____

   3) Describe the man's appearance.

      _____

      _____

   4) Relate how Francis tried to make himself comfortable.

      _____

      _____

   5) Describe the images that went through Francis' mind as the storm worsened.

      _____

      _____

3. Continue the story in any way you think fits in with the opening. Write for about five minutes. Try not to pause.

Exercise 3-23   Writing Topics (continued)

WRITING TOPIC

4. Recall an incident in your life when you felt safe and secure. Suddenly you noticed signs of danger. Recreate the circumstances that made you think you were safe to begin with. Then relate how these circumstances changed. How did you react to this change?

_____

_____

_____

_____

_____

_____

_____

_____

_____

_____

_____

_____

_____

_____

_____

_____

_____

_____

Exercise 3-24   Writing Topics

INSTRUCTIONS: Read the passage below, answer the questions that follow, and write and revise a composition on the given topic.

RESPONSIBILITY FOR OTHERS

Opening of James Baldwin's "Sonny's Blues" (taken from James Baldwin, *Going to Meet the Man,* published by The Dial Press, 1957).

[1]I read about it in the paper, in the subway, on my way to work. I read it, and I couldn't believe it, and I read it again. Then perhaps I just stared at it, at the newsprint spelling out his name, spelling out the story. I stared at it in the swinging lights of the subway car, and in the faces and bodies of the people, and in my own face, trapped in the darkness which roared outside. [2]It was not to be believed and I kept telling myself that, as I walked from the subway station to the high school. And at the same time I couldn't doubt it. I was scared, scared for Sonny. [3]He became real to me again. A great block of ice got settled in my belly and kept melting there slowly all day long, while I taught my classes algebra. It was a special kind of ice. It kept melting, sending trickles of ice water all up and down my veins, but it never got less. Sometimes it hardened and seemed to expand until I felt my guts were going to come spilling out or that I was going to choke or scream. [4]This would always be at a moment when I was remembering some specific thing Sonny had once said or done.

When he was about as old as the boys in my classes his face had been bright and open, there was a lot of copper in it; and he'd had wonderfully direct brown eyes, and great gentleness and privacy. [5]I wondered what he looked like now. He had been picked up, the evening before, in a raid on an apartment downtown, for peddling and using heroin. . . .

1.   The details in the opening passage of this story work together to recreate in the reader the way the storyteller felt on a particular occasion. In two or three sentences, describe that feeling.

_____

_____

_____

_____

2. The numbers 1 to 5 in the excerpt you just read correspond to the directions below. Following these directions, compose sentences that develop the story's opening further. Read your newly revised passage aloud to hear if it helps your reader imagine this scene a little differently. The first one is done for you.

   1) State what the newspaper headline said.

   <u>The headline seemed to scream, directly at</u>

   <u>me, ''Drug Raid Nets Twelve, Including</u>

   <u>Sonny!''</u>

   2) State how the speaker tried to keep himself from believing what he was reading in the newspaper.

   _____

   _____

   3) State in what way Sonny had been "unreal" for the speaker until he read the newspaper.

   _____

   _____

   4) Relate "one specific thing Sonny had once said or done" to pain the speaker.

   _____

   _____

   5) Describe how the speaker imagined Sonny looked now.

   _____

   _____

3. Continue the story in any way you think fits in with the opening. Write for about five minutes. Try not to pause.

Exercise 3-24 Writing Topics (continued)

WRITING TOPIC

4. Recall an incident in your life when you wanted to help someone very badly, but you knew that helping him or her would cause you problems. Explain how you were faced with such a situation and how you responded. Who was the person? What were the circumstances? What made you want to help the person? What did you want to do for him or her? How could helping the person have caused you problems? What kind of problems?

_____

_____

_____

_____

_____

_____

_____

_____

_____

_____

_____

_____

_____

_____

Exercise 3-25   Writing Topics

INSTRUCTIONS: Read the passage below, answer the questions that follow, and write and revise a composition on the given topic.

GOING OUT INTO THE WORLD

Opening of E. B. White's "The Second Tree from the Corner" (taken from E. B. White, *The Second Tree from the Corner*, published by Harper & Row, 1947).

[1]"Ever have any bizarre thoughts?" asked the doctor.

Mr. Trexler failed to catch the word. "What kind?" he said.

"Bizarre," repeated the doctor, his voice steady. He watched his patient for any slight change of expression, any wince. [2]It seemed to Trexler that the doctor was not only watching him closely but was creeping slowly toward him, like a lizard toward a bug. Trexler shoved his chair back an inch and gathered himself for a reply. [3]He was about to say "Yes" when he realized that if he said yes the next question would be unanswerable. Bizarre thoughts, bizarre thoughts? Ever have any bizarre thoughts? What kind of thoughts *except* bizarre had he had since the age of two?

[4]Trexler felt the time passing, the necessity for an answer. These psychiatrists were busy men, overloaded, not to be kept waiting. The next patient was probably already perched out there in the waiting room, lonely, worried, shifting around on the sofa, his mind stuffed with bizarre thoughts and amorphous fears. Poor bastard, thought Trexler. [5]Out there all alone in that misshapen antechamber, staring at the filing cabinet and wondering whether to tell the doctor about that day on the Madison Avenue bus. . . .

1. The comment of the storyteller and the thoughts of Mr. Trexler in the opening of this story give you an idea of what Mr. Trexler's attitude is toward the psychiatrist. Describe in two or three sentences what his attitude is.

_____

_____

_____

_____

2. The numbers 1 to 5 in the excerpt you just read correspond to the directions below. Following these directions, compose sentences that develop the story's opening further. Read your newly revised passage aloud to hear if the sentences you've written help your reader imagine this scene a little differently. The first one is done for you.

   1) Describe where the doctor is located in the room.

   ```
   Sitting behind a huge mahogany desk, the

   doctor leaned his elbows on the arms of his

   chair as he folded his hands in prayer

   underneath his chubby chin.
   ```

   2) Tell how else Trexler reacted to the doctor's seeming to creep toward him in addition to "inching" his chair back.

   _____

   _____

   3) Refer to one particularly bizarre thought that Trexler decided he certainly didn't want to tell the doctor.

   _____

   _____

   4) Tell how the doctor behaved as he waited for Trexler's answer.

   _____

   _____

   5) Relate what the doctor did to try to get Trexler to refocus on the business at hand.

   _____

   _____

Exercise 3-25   Writing Topics (continued)

3. Continue the story in any way you think fits in with the opening.
    Write for about five minutes. Do not pause for more than a few
    seconds at a time.

WRITING TOPIC

4. Recall a situation when you met with someone from whom you
    wanted some object or service, for example, someone whom you
    consulted for some reason or someone who interviewed you.
    Explain how successful or productive your meeting was and what
    made you think so. What was your purpose for meeting with the
    person? How did the person's actions and reactions and your
    actions and reactions make you think that your meeting was
    good—or not so good?

_____

_____

_____

_____

_____

_____

_____

_____

_____

_____

CHAPTER 4

MECHANICS

After you've revised your sentences to make sure that they work together to explain your paragraph's main idea, you or your readers might run into still another kind of obstacle. This kind of obstacle doesn't so much throw off your readers' understanding as much as it does temporarily distract them. This obstacle is composed of grammar and punctuation errors.

This aspect of writing is also called mechanics because it is concerned with the "machinery" of English—the rules that users of English have agreed to follow. Just as you must follow certain rules of adding, subtracting, multiplying, and dividing when you use numbers, you must follow certain rules of English if you want to make use of it for thinking, writing, and explaining. The higher-level uses of English allow you to think or analyze ideas. Similarly, the higher levels of mathematics are called analysis. Both kinds of languages require you to apply rules before they can be used successfully.

In writing it is possible to follow the rules of English mechanics without paying much attention to revising your ideas, but you will wind up with a weak paragraph that communicates very little, such as this example:

Yesterday we had a really great time at the beach. Everything seemed to be just perfect on a day just made for us. The weather was beautiful, the water just right, and the people there couldn't have been nicer. To make a long story short, it was a day I'll never forget. For having fun with friends, there's no place like the beach.

The writer has no trouble following grammar and punctuation rules. However, she must question the meanings of her words further in order to produce a more understandable explanation of what had been so wonderful about her day at the beach. Instead, what she has written is more like a series of unexplained generalizations that leaves readers wondering what she means.

Because this writer does not develop the implications of the points she makes, she's not so likely to stretch her writing and thinking enough to run into problems with mechanics. Revising for problems with mechanics must often wait until you've revised your paragraphs and sentences. Only after that are you ready to reread your sentences for any distractions caused by violating the grammar and punctuation rules of English.

The exercises in this section will allow you to practice following these grammar and punctuation rules (as well as a few others) by reading, combining, and completing sentences and paragraphs. Each sentence or paragraph makes use of rules and patterns discussed in this section. Perform the exercises as directed. There are both completion and combining exercises.

The completion exercises will involve you in (1) analyzing the meaning of the given rough draft, (2) thinking up words, phrases, and sentences that complete the meaning of the rough draft, and (3) applying grammar and punctuation rules.

The combining exercises require you to set up a variety of sentence structures. As you put together the meanings of the sentences and sentence parts, you will find yourself practicing structures that you listen to, speak, and read, but may not use in your own writing. The main point of the combining exercises, however, is to give you another opportunity of practicing the use of grammar and punctuation rules to enhance meaning.

Compare your answers with those of your writing partner. If you are unsure of any of these rules or patterns of meaning, return to the text explanation of them for review.

As far as possible, note how following each rule allows the meaning of the sentences you've completed or combined to show through more clearly. At the same time, notice how the sentences you've completed or combined incorrectly tend to confuse your reader.

WRITING COMPLETE SENTENCES

All writing is made up of sentences that allow you to make the points you need to make when you are thinking through or explaining an idea. A sentence names a person, place, or thing—its "subject"—and states what action the subject performed or how it is called or described—its "verb." For example:

The toddler whined.

The dandelion is yellow

The first rule to observe when writing is that every sentence must combine a subject and a predicate, which is made up of a verb and its complement, to state a complete thought. Sometimes in your writing, you may encounter a group of words that begins with a capital letter and ends with a period but does not make a complete statement, for example:

Especially the ripe apples, sweet grapes, and juicy plums.

Even after she had admitted that her dirty sneakers didn't belong there.

These unfinished thoughts that look like sentences but really are not are called *fragments*. They are really parts of unexpressed thoughts that have become detached from the main subject and verb needed for each. In these cases we can add "Tim admired" and "Rhoda refused" to make each a complete sentence:

Tim admired the fine fruits on display at the Farmer's Market, especially the ripe apples, sweet grapes, and juicy plums.

Rhoda refused to remove her gym clothes from the living room, even after she admitted that her dirty sneakers didn't belong there.

When you are rewriting and revising, if you come across a sentence that doesn't seem to express who or what it is talking about—the subject—or what is being said about the subject—the verb—you will become confused. You've encountered a fragment, such as:

Because he worked late last Saturday night.

The questioning technique you used when making the point of your paragraph and sentences clearer can be used to decide how to make the fragment into a complete thought. Ask questions about the words that confuse you:

What happened "because he worked late last Saturday night"?

Who did what "because he worked late last Saturday night"?

Here are a couple of possible answers:

Gerry slept until noon on Sunday because he worked late last Saturday night.

Gerry was late for his date with Trudy because he worked late last Saturday night.

We now have a subject—"Gerry"—and a verb—"slept" and "was"—to make sense of the details that complete their meaning.

Exercise 4-1   Avoiding Fragments

INSTRUCTIONS: Combine the sentences below by making use of only one of the listed words or phrases that precede them.

When combining the sentences, delete any unnecessary words. For example, when the following sentences are combined by means of the phrase "since she was," the phrase "Tracy was" is no longer necessary:

Tracy was exhausted from her aerobic dancing.
Tracy told her husband that she didn't have the strength to help him prepare dinner.

```
Since she was exhausted from her aerobic
dancing, Tracy told her husband that she didn't
have the strength to help him prepare dinner.
```

Or, you might have been asked to use only the word "exhausted" to combine these two ideas. In this case "Tracy was" is still unnecessary:

```
Exhausted from her aerobic dancing, Tracy told
her husband that she didn't have the strength
to help him prepare dinner.
```

The first one is done for you.

in order to	thinking	after
although	such as	

1. Nancy slammed the door.
   She had jammed two huge pizzas into the freezer.

   After she had jammed two huge pizzas into the
   freezer, Nancy slammed the door.

2. Edwina thought no one was looking.
   Edwina filled her plate for the third time at her sister's wedding reception.

   _____

   _____

_____

_____

3. Stan practiced solving equations for two hours every evening.
    Stan wanted to pass his math final.

_____

_____

_____

_____

4. Jane bakes many types of desserts.
    Some of these desserts are lemon meringue pie, devil's food cake,
    and peanut butter cookies.

_____

_____

_____

_____

5. Theodora had written her history term paper twice.
    Theodora wrote it once more before she handed it in.

_____

_____

_____

_____

| rejected | touched | since |
| after | including | |

6. Rowena's diet consists mostly of vegetables.
    Among the vegetables she eats are carrots, lima beans, and squash.

Exercise 4-1 Avoiding Fragments (continued)

_____

_____

_____

_____

7. My brother earned his Ph.D. in music from Oberlin College.
   He taught the history of music at State College.

_____

_____

_____

_____

8. Rollo's father hugged him affectionately.
   Rollo's father was touched by the beautiful watch Rollo had given
   him for his birthday.

_____

_____

_____

_____

9. Rick was rejected by the Army, the Navy, and the Air Force.
   Rick filled out an application for the French Foreign Legion.

_____

_____

_____

_____

10. Chad has never paid a bill on time in his life.
He has met every collection agent in the state of New Jersey.

_____

_____

_____

_____

Exercise 4-2   Avoiding Fragments

INSTRUCTIONS: Combine the following sentences by making use of one of the words or phrases from each list. The first one is done for you.

although	so that	as
whenever	except for	

1. The only exceptions are his light grey shoes and mauve argyle socks.
    Usually I admire whatever my husband wears.

    Usually I admire whatever my husband wears,

    except for his light grey shoes and mauve

    argyle socks.

2. Kathleen was able to enter it in the state kennel show.
    Kathleen paid a trainer twenty-five dollars an hour to teach her poodle tricks.

    _____

    _____

    _____

    _____

3. Bill refused to drop his French course.
    For half of the semester, Bill hasn't understood a word that his French instructor has spoken.

    _____

    _____

    _____

    _____

4. Pat worked at her office desk.
Pat coughed, sniffled, and shivered.

_____

_____

_____

_____

5. Ronnie runs out his back door.
Someone is ringing Ronnie's front door bell.

_____

_____

_____

_____

that   despite the fact that   who
spinning   so tightly that

6. My new boss squeezed my hand tightly.
Tears sprang to my eyes.

_____

_____

_____

_____

7. Theodore worked for my father for forty years.
Theodore inherited my father's plumbing business.

_____

_____

_____

_____

Exercise 4-2 Avoiding Fragments (continued)

8. I bought a thick book about movie stars.
   It was made up of too many words and not enough pictures.

   _____

   _____

   _____

   _____

9. Chuck has always admired his mother-in-law.
   His wife dislikes her.

   _____

   _____

   _____

   _____

10. The ballerina spun in countless circles.
    The ballerina appeared to be both still and moving at the same
    time.

   _____

   _____

   _____

   _____

Exercise 4-3　Avoiding Fragments

INSTRUCTIONS:　Read the following sentences carefully. If the sentence is a complete thought, place a period at the end of it. Then write another sentence that might very well come after it in a story or explanation. If the group of words does not state a complete thought, make it into a complete sentence by adding a subject and/or a verb and whatever additional words are needed to complete the meaning of the verb. The first one is done for you.

1. Throwing the ball directly at the batter

   <u>The pitcher threw the ball directly at the</u>

   <u>batter. The batter jumped back and mumbled</u>

   <u>something under his breath.</u>

2. Peter painted the backyard fence a bright shade of lavender

   _____

   _____

   _____

   _____

3. Until Charlene finishes waxing her motorcycle

   _____

   _____

   _____

   _____

4. In order to wrap Jack's birthday gift without his knowing about it

   _____

   _____

5. The algebra student ripped the sheet of paper right out of her notebook

_____

_____

_____

_____

6. Disturbed but not wanting to show it

_____

_____

_____

_____

7. In addition to apples, pears, plums, and grapes

_____

_____

_____

_____

8. Ringing up the records her customer wanted to buy

_____

_____

_____

_____

Exercise 4-3   Avoiding Fragments (continued)

9. While filling out his income tax forms, Ron used up half a dozen pencils and three calculator batteries

_____

_____

_____

_____

10. Because Rhoda had never dreamed her stepfather would pay for her summer in Europe

_____

_____

_____

_____

11. No matter what he says about his bowling average

_____

_____

_____

_____

Exercise 4-4   Avoiding Fragments

INSTRUCTIONS: Read the following sentences carefully. If the sentence is a complete thought, place a period at the end of it. Then write another sentence that might very well come after it in a story or explanation. If the group of words does not state a complete thought, make it into a complete sentence by adding a subject and/or a verb and whatever additional words are needed to complete the meaning of the verb. The first one is done for you.

1.   Except for the three-pound box of chocolates that Max had given her

     Except for the three-pound box of chocolates
     that Max had given her, Amanda wasn't excited
     about any of the birthday presents she had
     received.

2.   Besides the pink, bloody hamburgers and the cold, greasy French fries

     _____

     _____

     _____

     _____

3.   The boxer wearing the tartan trunks cornered his opponent

     _____

     _____

     _____

     _____

4. Frowning at the sound she heard coming from her instrument, the violinist paused to tighten one of her strings

_____

_____

_____

_____

5. In order to graduate from high school, Sam needed to attend school during the summer

_____

_____

_____

_____

6. Relaxed, and grinning from ear to ear,

_____

_____

_____

_____

7. In addition to the pants and shirts he has already tried on

_____

_____

_____

_____

Exercise 4-4   Avoiding Fragments (continued)

8. Professor Ramirez warned his students to hand in only typewritten essays

_____

_____

_____

_____

9. The jelly doughnut felt like a lump in Wayne's otherwise empty stomach

_____

_____

_____

_____

10. Unfortunately, Jerry's stained tie, wrinkled shirt, and dull shoes

_____

_____

_____

_____

Exercise 4-5   Avoiding Fragments

INSTRUCTIONS: Read the following groups of words in each item below very carefully. If the group of words is a complete thought, capitalize the first word. Then write a sentence that could come before it in a story or explanation. The first one is done for you.

1.   she especially enjoyed trigonometry and calculus.

Tess had always been fascinated by

mathematics. She especially enjoyed

trigonometry and calculus.

2.   especially his socks, shoes, and underwear.

_____

_____

_____

_____

3.   despite what his wife says about him.

_____

_____

_____

_____

4.   he, too, believed that his writing had improved greatly.

_____

_____

_____

_____

5. playing her guitar and reading murder mysteries occupied her for several hours each day.

_____

_____

_____

_____

6. for example, she shouted at the mail carrier and cursed at the television set.

_____

_____

_____

_____

7. otherwise, I'd have to pay twelve percent interest.

_____

_____

_____

_____

8. also, she threw the diamond brooch in my face.

_____

_____

_____

_____

Exercise 4-5   Avoiding Fragments (continued)

9. it contained gin, vodka, bourbon, and rye.

_____

_____

_____

_____

10. which tasted very hot and spicy.

_____

_____

_____

11. such as the point of view that parents owe their children a college education.

_____

_____

_____

_____

Exercise 4-6   Avoiding Fragments

INSTRUCTIONS: Read the following paragraphs aloud. Place a period at the end of each complete thought and capital letters at the beginning of sentences. The first sentence is done for you.

1. When Linda was twelve-years-old, she loved to visit her Uncle Lewis' farm in Western Pennsylvania. The day after school let out, usually around the twentieth of June, Linda's father would drive the three hundred miles from her home in Pennsylvania to Uncle Lewis' two-hundred-acre home right on the Ohio border Linda enjoyed many things about staying with Uncle Lewis, but at the top of the list was the fact that the Renfroes and their thirteen-year-old son Rob lived only a half-mile away she and Rob had become inseparable during the summer together they enjoyed activities that Linda would never have gotten to do back home in Carthage best of all, her parents weren't there to tell her what to do, when to do it, and how to do it

2. Linda and Rob especially loved to fish before coming to Uncle Lewis', Linda had hated fishing her father and her three older brothers would force her to go fishing with them in a muddy, polluted river near their home after squishing night crawlers on her hook, she would throw her line into the water and stare at the steel-company smoke stacks on the other side of the river meanwhile her brothers teased her for not catching any fish fishing with Rob was quite different Linda and he would spend an entire sunny day at a crystal-clear pond about a mile from Rob's house the pond was surrounded by pasture land that seemed golden in the sun the pond even provided a huge chestnut tree to protect fishermen and swimmers alike from the midday sun

COMBINING RELATED SENTENCES

Sentences should work together to support a paragraph's main idea. For the most part they accomplish this by stating causes, effects, and examples implied in the paragraph's topic sentence. (See "Paragraph Logic.") As you draw out these supporting statements, you must be careful to state them one at a time, or, if they're doing similar explaining work, you can join them together in *compound sentences*.

A compound sentence is a sentence that joins together two separate and independent thoughts such as:

The wind whistled down the chimney, and the windows rattled.

Notice how each subject-verb combination—"wind whistled" and "windows rattled"—can be understood separately in its own sentence:

The wind whistled down the chimney.

The windows rattled.

As you unfold the implied meanings of the words and ideas in your rough draft, your experience with spoken English will influence you to make use of the compound sentence, for example, when presenting two equally important pieces of evidence to explain a general point:

Last New Year's Eve in my grandfather's mountain cabin was not as cozy as I had imagined it would be. The wind whistled down the chimney, and the windows rattled. I could hear mice making crackling noises under the drafty floorboards, so I lay motionless on an uncomfortable cot, waiting for the morning light.

Such compounded thoughts are connected by the words *and, but, nor, or, for, yet*, and *so*. Because these words join ideas together, they are called *conjunctions*. When these words are used to connect complete thoughts, they must have a comma in front of them, as if you've joined the thoughts with the conjunction while keeping them independent and separate by means of the comma.

As a reader, you can sense that this comma rule has been violated when you find yourself in the middle of an idea before you've really understood the idea that preceded it, for instance:

I thought about deserting my friend Elena sleeping on a cot on the other side of the cabin but I didn't know where I'd desert to.

Readers ought to have the opportunity of understanding the first thought before considering how it's joined to the next one, so a comma must be placed before the "but":

I thought about deserting my friend Elena sleeping on a cot on the other side of the cabin, but I didn't know where I'd desert to.

Not placing a comma in front of the *and, but, nor, or, for, yet,* or *so* produces the error known as a *run-on* or *run-together sentence.*

Another way to avoid writing run-on sentences when you are combining two complete sentences is with a semicolon (;). When the relationship you want to emphasize between the two combined thoughts is not made clear by *and, but, nor, or, for, yet,* or *so,* you can connect the two sentences with a semicolon instead of a comma and conjunction. For example: these two sentences

Herb had finally passed English.
He was now a high school graduate.

can be combined with a semicolon like this:

Herb had finally passed English; he was now a high school graduate.

NAME _____

Exercise 4-7 Avoiding Run-ons

INSTRUCTIONS: Each pair of sentences below implies a relationship. Use *and, but, nor, or, for, yet,* or *so* if one of these conjunctions makes clearest the relationship that exists between the two thoughts. Remember to put a comma in front of the conjunction. If none of these words makes the relationship clear, use a semicolon instead. The first one is done for you.

1. Ernie turned on the television to watch the Sixer's game.
   The game had been canceled.

   <u>Ernie turned on the television to watch the</u>

   <u>Sixer's game, but the game had been canceled.</u>

2. The chef burned the roast beef.
   The customer ate it anyway.

   _____

   _____

   _____

   _____

   _____

3. The dental technician carefully cleaned my teeth.
   The dentist filled my cavities.

   _____

   _____

   _____

   _____

   _____

4. Leon missed composition class for the fifth time.
The instructor withdrew him from the class.

_____

_____

_____

_____

5. The buzzer on my clock radio went off at exactly six o'clock.
It startled me out of a sound sleep.

_____

_____

_____

_____

6. Leslie will soon have to find a full-time job.
Her parents will throw her out of the house.

_____

_____

_____

_____

7. Be wise as the serpent.
Be innocent as the dove.

_____

_____

_____

_____

Exercise 4-7 Avoiding Run-ons (continued)

8. The sound coming from the television set was garbled.
    The picture was sharp.

    _____

    _____

    _____

    _____

9. Sylvia was beautiful, witty, and talented.
    Also she was a millionaire.

    _____

    _____

    _____

    _____

10. Fran realized she hadn't paid for the nail polish she had taken from
    Woolworth's.
    As a result, she returned it.

    _____

    _____

    _____

    _____

11. I like coffee for breakfast.
    My sister likes tea.

    _____

    _____

Exercise 4-8 Avoiding Run-ons

INSTRUCTIONS: Each pair of sentences below implies a relationship. Use *and, but, nor, or, for, yet,* or *so* if one of these conjunctions makes clearest the relationship that exists between the two thoughts. Remember to put a comma in front of the conjunction. If none of these conjunctions makes the relationship clear, use a semicolon instead. The first one is done for you.

1. Hanna and her sisters reluctantly went to the party.
   They had lots of fun anyway.

   Hanna and her sisters reluctantly went to the

   party, but they had lots of fun anyway.

2. Rhonda and Eve greeted one another with hugs and kisses.
   They hadn't seen one another for several years.

   _____

   _____

   _____

   _____

3. A bus ride to school costs a dollar while a taxi ride costs five dollars.
   I've decided to take the bus.

   _____

   _____

   _____

   _____

4. Joy prepared breakfast for her three children. Next she made their lunches.

_____

_____

_____

_____

5. I'm the worst basketball player in my neighborhood. In fact, I've never shot a basket.

_____

_____

_____

_____

6. Please clear the dishes off the kitchen table. Otherwise, we'll have flies in the house.

_____

_____

_____

_____

7. All the lilies in our flower garden are wilted. I'm watering them.

_____

_____

_____

_____

Exercise 4-8 Avoiding Run-ons (continued)

8. Jake ordered his six-year-old son Lance to wash his hands. Instead, Lance turned on the faucet as he wiped his hands on the towel.

_____

_____

_____

_____

9. Pete brushes his hair at least once an hour. He thinks all the women in his office are always staring at him.

_____

_____

_____

_____

10. "Start studying," the coach shouted at the members of the basketball team. "You'll all be ineligible to play next semester."

_____

_____

_____

_____

11. Jill carefully added hues of blue to her seascape. She thought it didn't look mysterious enough.

_____

_____

Exercise 4-9   Avoiding Run-ons

INSTRUCTIONS: Put periods, commas, and semicolons in the paragraphs below wherever they're needed. Make sure each sentence is a complete thought, and make sure you show the connection between the two related thoughts (a) by placing a comma in front of *and, but, nor, or, for, yet,* or *so;* (b) by placing a semicolon between them; or (c) by putting a period at the end of one sentence and a capital at the beginning of the next sentence. The first sentence is done for you.

1.   Maria had finally gotten up the courage to return to school; she was certainly glad she had. She was now forty and ever since she had graduated from high school and failed to find a job that stimulated her, she had wanted to return to school to study nursing she knew she had begun to travel a long, difficult road she really hadn't paid much attention to math or biology or English while in high school she hadn't even bothered to sign up for chemistry, thinking it was too much work for somebody who just wanted to graduate, own a new car, and live in an elegantly furnished apartment she discovered that things didn't come so easily.

2.   After high school, she earned enough money as a secretary to buy an expensive car and to rent a modest apartment but the apartment wasn't very nicely furnished at all she certainly had no money left over from her paycheck to buy nice clothes or occasionally to eat out at a restaurant not only could she not afford these things, it gradually dawned on her that she wasn't able to make her job as interesting as it might be if she had studied and thought more while she was in high school Alice, her next door neighbor, seemed to enjoy her work as a nurse also she seemed to have interesting things to say and ideas to express that Maria had never even thought of at forty Maria needed no further evidence to convince her that she belonged back in school or was it that she belonged in school for the very first time?

Exercise 4-10 Avoiding Run-ons

INSTRUCTIONS: Read each item below carefully. Then use one of the listed words or phrases to compose a related sentence that makes sense joined with the given sentence. Remember to use a comma in front of *and, but, nor, or, for, yet,* and *so* when they join two complete sentences. Otherwise use either a period or a semicolon to separate your new sentence from the given one. The first one is done for you.

as a result	at the same time	yet
nor	also	so

1. Jake ran out of paper while writing his composition

    Jake ran out of paper while writing his
    composition, so he borrowed some from Ida
    sitting right next to him.

2. Miguel refinishes furniture so that it looks like new

    _____

    _____

    _____

    _____

    _____

3. In the winter my feet always feel cold

    _____

    _____

    _____

    _____

    _____

4. Bertha cut the vegetables for the stew

_____

_____

_____

_____

5. The coffee was tepid and the cream curdled

_____

_____

_____

_____

6. Jack hasn't yet gotten his hair cut

_____

_____

_____

_____

| it | so | he |
| and | but | |

7. Hank hadn't had his car tuned up for two years

_____

_____

_____

_____

Exercise 4-10 Avoiding Run-ons (continued)

8. Lucy dances better than anyone in her ballet class

_____

_____

_____

_____

9. I was astounded when I finally saw the Grand Canyon

_____

_____

_____

_____

10. Mr. Foley, who owned half of the real estate in our town, died without a will

_____

_____

_____

_____

11. Bobby brought the beer, potato chips, and pretzels to our Super Bowl party

_____

_____

_____

Exercise 4-11 Avoiding Run-ons

INSTRUCTIONS: Read each item below carefully. Then use one of the listed words or phrases to compose a related sentence that makes sense joined with the given sentence. Remember to use a comma in front of *and, but, nor, or, for, yet,* or *so* when they join two complete sentences. Otherwise use either a period or a semicolon to separate your new sentence from the given one. The first one is done for you.

or	instead	it
there	so	as a result

1. The pot of yellow mums on the radiator had dried up

    The pot of yellow mums on the radiator had

    dried up; as a result, Father threw them out.

2. Kirby threw the burned toast, runny egg, and charred bacon into the garbage

    _____

    _____

    _____

    _____

    _____

3. Lara had not phoned her boss to tell her that she wouldn't be reporting for work today

    _____

    _____

    _____

    _____

4. The campers were afraid to enter the cave they had discovered

_____

_____

_____

_____

5. During the loudest part of the song, the guitarist played the wrong chord

_____

_____

_____

_____

6. After graduating from high school, Mary may join the Air Force

_____

_____

_____

_____

I   for   therefore
so   also

7. During a phone conversation with my lawyer, I slammed down the receiver

_____

_____

_____

_____

Exercise 4-11 Avoiding Run-ons (continued)

8. Until I took my American History II course, I had never realized that religious persecution caused many early settlers to come to America

_____

_____

_____

_____

9. Magdalena had already read one historian's account of the French Revolution

_____

_____

_____

_____

10. Jennifer chose to wear sneakers to the prom

_____

_____

_____

_____

11. "Please excuse Mildred for being a half-hour late for class

_____

_____

_____

Exercise 4-12   Avoiding Run-ons

INSTRUCTIONS: Read each item below carefully. Then use one of the listed words or phrases to compose a related sentence that makes sense joined with the given sentence. Remember to use a comma in front of *and, but, nor, or, for, yet,* or *so* when they join two complete sentences. Otherwise use either a period or a semicolon to separate your new sentence from the given one. The first one is done for you.

also	and	in fact
instead	meanwhile	or

1. _____ she will be asked to resign from her bowling league.

   <u>Gerry must raise her average to a hundred, or</u>

   <u>she will be asked to resign from her bowling</u>

   <u>league.</u>

2. _____ the goalie had knocked George's teeth out.

   _____

   _____

   _____

   _____

3. _____ then he sprayed the house plants with a fine mist.

   _____

   _____

   _____

   _____

4. _____ his watch dog ripped the seat right out of his pants.

_____

_____

_____

_____

5. _____ he memorized the meaning of every technical term in the chapter.

_____

_____

_____

_____

6. _____ he cut the grapefruit in half with a pair of scissors.

_____

_____

_____

_____

| so | instead | or |
| they | but | |

7. _____ her serve is very awkward.

_____

_____

_____

_____

Exercise 4-12 Avoiding Run-ons (continued)

8. _____ he had to have them dry cleaned.

_____

_____

_____

9. _____ he read comic books and ate jujubes.

_____

_____

_____

10. _____ were doomed never to marry.

_____

_____

_____

11. _____ Eleanor will resign from her position
as mayor.

_____

_____

_____

USING -*s* AND -*ed* ENDINGS ON VERBS

Another set of rules to be observed if the meanings of your words are to be clearly understandable concerns verb forms. We all belong to specialized groups of English speakers who have developed their own rules when speaking to one another. This is often most noticeable in the forms of verbs we use. One student, speaking casually to another student, for example, might make use of these underlined verb forms:

I <u>says</u> to the coach, I had <u>went</u> to practice everyday, but he still <u>tell</u> me I off the team. I <u>complain</u> to the dean but he says he <u>have</u> to look into it.

I <u>drag</u> myself out of bed this morning when the phone had <u>rang</u>. I <u>seen</u> that nobody was at home, so I <u>run</u> downstairs to answer it. When I had <u>come</u> down the stairs, I <u>trips</u> over a dogs bone.

However, when you're writing a document to be read by many people, you must observe the rules that English speakers from many different backgrounds have agreed upon. This especially applies to verbs, since the verb is the part of the sentence that turns the subject into a statement or idea.

Two crucial rules to follow for *regular verbs* are (1) to use an -*s* ending when you're saying something about a he, she, or it subject in the present and (2) to use an -*ed* ending when you're stating that your subject did something in the past:

Every afternoon Manny lif<u>ts</u> weights for two hours before going to work.

After Manny came home from work last night, he lift<u>ed</u> weights for another hour.

Note the conditions that apply here. In the first sentence the writer is making a point about a *he* subject, "Manny" (a third-person, singular form), and his lifting weights is going on in the present. In the second sentence, Manny's coming home took place in the past ("last night"), so an -*ed* is needed on the word "lift" to show that the lifting is over and done with too.

When you write a paragraph relating a series of events that took place in the past, you must put an -*ed* on the verbs to keep the tense consistent throughout, for example:

Late in my senior year of high school, I decid<u>ed</u> to apply for admission to college for several reasons. I realiz<u>ed</u> that I need<u>ed</u> to know more if I want<u>ed</u> to pursue a career in telecommunications. . . .

Finally, make sure that you attach an *-ed* to the verb form used with helping verbs like *has, have,* and *had.* This verb form is called the *past participle*:

Mr. Grim, my supervisor, <u>has promoted</u> me to assistant manager.

Tess' squash pie <u>was awarded</u> a sixth-place ribbon at the county fair.

Exercise 4-13   Putting -*s* and -*ed* Endings on Verbs

INSTRUCTIONS: Read the sentence carefully in each item below to determine whether the action is taking place in the present or the past. Then combine the words following the sentence into a complete sentence. Remember to put either -*s* or -*ed* on the verb of the sentence you construct. The first one is done for you.

1.   Writing is one of the most difficult and fulfilling activities humankind pursues.
in order / (write) / to live / a human being

   A human being writes in order to live.
   _____

2.   Bob never does his homework for algebra class.
yesterday's / (fail) / he / to no one's surprise / pop quiz

   _____

   _____

3.   My four-year-old brother is the boss in our house.
on television / what programs we watch / (decide) / he

   _____

   _____

4.   My boss has a wicked temper.
I have / to get along / (manage) / so far / with her / however

   _____

   _____

5.   Roberta's husband announced he was tired of paying high energy bills.
Roberta / he / to turn off the heat / (ask) / while she's at home alone

   _____

   _____

6. Everything on the menu seems very appetizing.
   of the Peking Duck / (look) / the photograph / delicious / especially

   _____

   _____

7. Dr. Rowe must improve his penmanship.
   when he wrote "fourteen" / (charge) / me / his receptionist / forty
   dollars

   _____

   _____

8. Todd misses living in California.
   the streets of Trenton / (wander) / he / every Saturday / carrying a
   surfboard and looking for a beach

   _____

   _____

9. Elsa is serving a five-year sentence in Leesburg prison.
   of income-tax / she / was / evasion / (convict)

   _____

   _____

10. Michele ironed her red flannel shirt very carefully.
    to her friend Elsa's / (invite) / she / engagement party / had been

    _____

    _____

11. "When will Mr. Ruddman stop giving us these foolish exercises?"
    one of his composition students asked another.
    "the only course / he / is his / we're taking / (think)"

    _____

    _____

Exercise 4-14   Putting *-s* and *-ed* Endings on Verbs

INSTRUCTIONS: Read the sentence carefully in each item below to determine whether the action is taking place in the present or the past. Then combine the words following the sentence into a complete sentence. Remember to put either *-s* or *-ed* on the verb of the sentence you construct. The first one is done for you.

1. Jack denied that he had ever made such a nasty remark to his cat Moll.
    that he has / soothingly / he (insist) / always (talk) / to her

    He insisted that he has always talked
    _____

    soothingly to her.
    _____

2. Mother congratulated me on having earned my associate's degree in computer science.
    my diploma / (cry) / as he studied / Father

    _____

    _____

    _____

3. James had just broken his leg in two places.
    the stairs / very / he / (climb) / slowly / to his room

    _____

    _____

    _____

4. I received a "D" in typing my final semester in high school.
    (accept) / by Yale / I / but / not by Harvard / was

    _____

    _____

    _____

5. Seventy-five-year-old Mr. Rosado plans to travel around the world when he reaches the age of eighty.
by collecting old newspapers / he / to finance / (plan) / and scrap metal / his trip

_____

_____

6. Everyone could hear Myrna's teeth rattling during chemistry class this morning.
in the winter / that often / when she / (happen) / to put on / (forget) / her long underwear

_____

_____

7. Rex, whose vocabulary was very well developed, couldn't understand why he had received a "B" on his twelve-page research paper.
"you" / "over" / "(trip)" / "too often" / "your big words," / (explain) / Mrs. Beaseley

_____

_____

8. Rachel never seems to be able to make a decision.
everything / (ponder) / as if / a life-or-death situation / she / it's

_____

_____

9. Ms. Grinch denies that she ever agreed to marry Mr. Havershaw.
however / that / Mr. Havershaw / (insist) / she did

_____

_____

Exercise 4-14   Putting *-s* and *-ed* Endings on Verbs

10. My army physical was one of the most embarrassing experiences of my life.
    never again / into a small room / will I be / with forty men / (crowd) / wearing only undershorts

    _____

    _____

11. Every night Mrs. Lutz prays for her fifty-year-old twin sons.
    marry / she / they / (hope) / will soon

    _____

    _____

Exercise 4-15 Putting -s and -ed Endings on Verbs

INSTRUCTIONS: Read the sentence carefully in each item below to discover whether the action is taking place in the present or in the past. Then use the supplied subject and verb (in parentheses) to write another sentence that might follow it in a composition or story. Make sure to put the proper -s or -ed ending on each verb.

1. Little Tina banged on the typewriter till she had broken every key.

    Her mother (spank) _____

    <u>Her mother spanked her and sent her to bed</u>

    <u>without any supper.</u>

2. Joey slammed the front door shut. Paint chips (drop) _____

    _____

    _____

3. In Newtown dogs aren't allowed on the sidewalk. Nevertheless,

    Jane (sneak) _____

    _____

    _____

4. My toddler has been sneezing and coughing for the last two hours.

    She (sound) _____

    _____

    _____

5. Martha wears a fox stole and diamonds when she goes to the

    supermarket. She (dress) _____

    _____

6. My pet hamster Samuel is a vicious little animal. He (bite) _____

_____

7. Jeff was quite nervous about his interview with the vice president
of People's Bank. He (change) _____

_____

8. Tim squeezed his pregnant wife's hand while she suffered another
contraction. He (encourage) _____

_____

9. Rhoda hadn't seen her college friend Georgina since Rhoda had
gotten married. They (chat) _____

_____

10. The annual recital was only two weeks away. Ned (practice) _____

_____

11. Lee's penmanship is impossible to decipher. He (type) _____

_____

Exercise 4-16   Putting *-s* and *-ed* Endings on Verbs

INSTRUCTIONS: Read the sentence in each item below to discover whether the action is taking place in the present or in the past. Then use the supplied subject and verb (in parentheses) to write another sentence that might follow it in a composition or story. Make sure to put the proper *-s* or *-ed* ending on each verb.

1. Yesterday Randy worked two eight-hour shifts at the factory. Today

    he (feel) _____

    <u>Today he feels too tired to get out of bed.</u>

2. Ten inches of snow had fallen during the night. I (pull) _____

    _____

    _____

3. Tommy knew he shouldn't be reading in bed so late at night. He

    (surrender) _____

    _____

    _____

4. Dr. Ricardo was about to give Jamie his flue shot. Jamie (stiffen)

    _____

    _____

5. Only eight ounces of beer remained in the pitcher. The thirsty bride

    (empty) _____

    _____

    _____

6. She had not eaten for at least two hours. The hungry baby (bang)

   _____

   _____

7. You can always tell when Irene has had too much to drink. She

   (lean) _____

   _____

   _____

8. My counselor is never shocked by anything I tell him. He (listen)

   _____

   _____

9. Every morning Artie has trouble putting in his contact lenses. He

   (blink) _____

   _____

   _____

10. Usually Archibald visits his mother on Thanksgiving. Then his

    mother (stay) _____

    _____

    _____

11. Percy is worried about having too many hormones. He (shave)

    _____

    _____

Exercise 4-17   Putting -*s* and -*ed* Endings on Verbs

INSTRUCTIONS: Read the sentence in each item below to discover whether the action is taking place in the present or in the past. Then use the supplied subject and verb (in parentheses) to write another sentence that might precede it in a composition or story. Make sure to put the proper -*s* or -*ed* ending on each verb.

1. George (impress) <u>impressed all his friends at</u>

   <u>school with his new muscular physique.</u>

   He had worked out at the gym every day during the summer.

2. Peter (loiter) _____

   _____

   _____

   He thought if he waited long enough someone would give him some money to buy an ice cream cone.

3. Jed often (dump) _____

   _____

   _____

   He'll try anything to improve the taste of his soup.

4. My heart (thump) _____

   _____

   _____

   I've always had a great fear of hospitals.

5. Zelda (stab) _____

   _____

   _____

She still wasn't able to get it opened.

6. The bicycle (rust) _____

_____

_____

Michael's parents refused to buy him another.

7. Fred often (trick) _____

_____

_____

He doesn't seem to be able to ask for what he wants.

8. My secretary (contradict) _____

_____

_____

He acts as if I'm a complete dope.

9. We (hope) _____

_____

_____

She had already flunked out of several small New England colleges.

10. Pedro carefully (preserve) _____

_____

_____

He hadn't won any awards since then.

Exercise 4-18   Putting "-s" and "-ed" Endings on Verbs

INSTRUCTIONS: Read the following paragraphs carefully. In the space next to the verbs in parentheses, write in the correct verb form called for. The first two have been done for you.

1.   Rex had always had trouble getting an "A" on a composition from Ms. Richards, his English teacher. He just could not figure out what

she (want) (1) __wanted__ . He (try) (2) __tried__ using lots of big phrases like so-and-so "proceeded to accomplish his objectives."

Ms. Richards only (remark) (3) _____ that those words

(seem) (4) _____ to get in the way of what he really

(intend) (5) _____ to say. Then he (compose)

(6) _____ his essays using little words like so-and-so "started to go to do his thing." Ms. Richards then said she was

terribly (confuse) (7) _____ as to what "thing" so-and-so

"did." Rex next (plan) (8) _____ to double the number of

words he had written in his rough draft; he then (use) (9) _____ time recopying the words in the neatest handwriting he could

manage. Ms. Richards (confess) (10) _____ that the words

on the page looked very pretty and that Rex had (double) (11) _____ the prettiness of the rough draft, which was only half as long

as the composition, but she also (acknowledge) (12) _____

that Rex's sentences (repeat) (13) _____ points already

made earlier in his composition. She also (point) (14) _____ out, sadly, that the sentences that (fail) (15) _____ to repeat points instead made irrelevant points.

2.   Rex can't figure out what Professor Richards wants. He has

(compose) (1) _____ long words, short words, long
sentences, short sentences, long paragraphs, short paragraphs, and
even pretty paragraphs; nothing has (work) (2) _____. He

doesn't know what to try next. He (decide) (3) _____ to ask

her, although he (remember) (4) _____ that the professor

has often (remind) (5) _____ the class what she (look)

(6) _____ for in their compositions. Then he is (inspire)

(7) _____ by a better idea. He will look again at the samples
of "A" compositions which Ms. Richards has (distribute)

(8) _____ to the class. Those should tell him something.

   He (read) (9) _____ them very carefully; he (look)

(10) _____ at them very attentively. First he (notice)

(11) _____ that the writer of an "A" essay never (worry)

(12) _____ whether a word is long or short, only if it (help)

(13) _____ state a clear and specific point. He then (observe)

(14) _____ another aspect of an "A" writer's work: every

sentence (develop) (15) _____ the point made in the

sentence before it. And he almost (faint) (16) _____

when he (realize) (17) _____ that every sentence (hint)

(18) _____ at what kind of point is going to be (handle)

(19) _____ in the sentence following it. For Rex, who is
studying to be an architect, this architecting of ideas is too
wonderful to believe.

USING IRREGULAR VERBS

As was discussed in the previous section, a writer must be careful to put -s or -ed on regular verbs in order to let the reader know that an action is taking place in the present or the past, as in:

Jean laughs heartily whenever she watches a Three Stooges movie.

Jean laughed heartily when she watched a Three Stooges movie last night.

Other verbs, called *irregular* verbs, do not use the -ed ending in the past tense. Instead they use unpredictable forms in the past tense and for the past participle when combined with helping verbs like *have*, *has*, or *had*. The following is a list of commonly used irregular verbs:

Present	Past	Past Participle
arise	arose	arisen
awake	awoke or awaked	awoke or awaked
be (am, are, is)	was (were)	been
bear	bore	born
become	became	become
begin	began	begun
bend	bent	bent
bite	bit	bitten
blow	blew	blown
break	broke	broken
bring	brought	brought
build	built	built
burst	burst	burst
buy	bought	bought
catch	caught	caught
choose	chose	chosen
come	came	come
cost	cost	cost
cut	cut	cut
dig	dug	dug
do (does)	did	done
drag	dragged	dragged

Present	Past	Past Participle
draw	drew	drawn
drink	drank	drunk
drive	drove	driven
drown	drowned	drowned
eat	ate	eaten
fall	fell	fallen
feed	fed	fed
feel	felt	felt
fight	fought	fought
find	found	found
fly	flew	flown
freeze	froze	frozen
get	got	got or gotten
give	gave	given
go (goes)	went	gone
grow	grew	grown
hang	hung	hung
hang	hanged	hanged
have (has)	had	had
hear	heard	heard
hide	hid	hidden
hold	held	held
hurt	hurt	hurt
keep	kept	kept
know	knew	known
lay	laid	laid
lead	led	led
leave	left	left
lend	lent	lent
let	let	let
lie	lay	lain
light	lit	lit
lose	lost	lost

Present	Past	Past Participle
make	made	made
meet	met	met
pay	paid	paid
ride	rode	ridden
ring	rang	rung
rise	rose	risen
run	ran	run
say	said	said
see	saw	seen
sell	sold	sold
send	sent	sent
set	set	set
shake	shook	shaken
shine	shone	shone
shine (polish)	shined	shined
shrink	shrank	shrunk
shut	shut	shut
sing	sang	sung
sink	sank	sunk
sit	sat	sat
sleep	slept	slept
sneak	sneaked	sneaked
speak	spoke	spoken
speed	sped	sped
spend	spent	spent
spring	sprang	sprung
stand	stood	stood
steal	stole	stolen
stick	stuck	stuck
sting	stung	stung
swear	swore	sworn
swim	swam	swum
swing	swang	swung

Present	Past	Past Participle
take	took	taken
teach	taught	taught
tear	tore	torn
tell	told	told
think	thought	thought
throw	threw	thrown
wake	woke or waked	woken or waked
wear	wore	worn
win	won	won
write	wrote	written

If you use one of these verbs in the present tense, you must use the form from the first column with the *-s* ending for a he, she, or it subject:

I <u>grow</u> fonder and fonder of playing soccer.
Tommy <u>grows</u> fonder and fonder of playing soccer.

If you use one of these verbs in the past tense, you must use the forms from the second column only:

I <u>grew</u> fonder and fonder of playing soccer.
Tommy <u>grew</u> fonder and fonder of playing soccer.

If you use one of these verbs with a helping verb, you must use the form from the third column only:

I <u>have grown</u> fonder and fonder of playing soccer.
Tommy <u>has grown</u> fonder and fonder of playing soccer.

Exercise 4-19   Using Irregular Verbs

INSTRUCTIONS: Read the sentence carefully in each item below to determine whether the action is taking place in the present or the past. Then combine the words following the sentence into a second sentence, making sure that you write the correct form of the verb in parentheses. Find the verb in the list provided or in a dictionary if you're not sure what form is called for. The first one is done for you.

1. The boxers squared off for twelve rounds.
    countless punches / they / trying / (throw) / to knock / one another / out

    They threw countless punches, trying to knock
    _____

    one another out.
    _____

2. I planned to ask my boss for a raise.
    my courage / I / when I noticed / (lose) / he was snarling

    _____

    _____

3. I can't afford to buy a video cassette recorder.
    to do / I've / for the time being / (choose) / without it

    _____

    _____

4. Henry's jacket was made of very porous material.
    when gusts / (blow) / of wind / (shake) / he / uncontrollably

    _____

    _____

5. The entire audience jammed their index fingers into their ears.
    in different keys / (sing) / the members / "God Bless America" / of the glee club

    _____

    _____

6. "Don't forget your lunch!" my father warned.
    "You have / to school / without it / (go) / every day this week"

    _____

    _____

7. Jimmy couldn't go anywhere without his music box.
    without food / he / but / could have / not without his music
    box / (go)

    _____

    _____

8. Geraldine always complains of cold feet.
    woolen / on the Fourth of July / she / (wear) / even / has / socks

    _____

    _____

9. The clerk in the unemployment office signaled to me to sit down.
    and (sit) down / I / to the chair / (come) / up / in front of his desk

    _____

    _____

10. Marvin moaned as he held his stomach.
    he was sorry / a gallon / he / had / of orange-ade / (drink)

    _____

    _____

11. His brother Mortimer grinned with pleasure.
    a third / (eat) / he / hot fudge sundae / gulped down / although
    he / already / two of them / had

    _____

    _____

Exercise 4-20   Using Irregular Verbs

INSTRUCTIONS: Read the sentence carefully in each item below to determine whether the action is taking place in the present or the past. Then combine the words following the sentence into a second sentence, making sure that you write the correct form of the verb in parentheses. Find the verb in the list provided or in a dictionary if you are not sure what form is called for. The first one is done for you.

1. Jerome denied that he had ever said such a thing to his friend.
    his temper / that he had / he insisted / not / during the argument / (lose)

    He insisted that he had not lost his temper

    during the argument.

2. May and Joe were unsure what they should prepare for their dinner guests.
    the roast beef / was / that they had / (take) / (freeze) / out of the refrigerator / still

    _____

    _____

    _____

3. I reported the details to the police as best I could.
    someone / out of / had / my bedroom / (steal) / all of my souvenir / menus / restaurant

    _____

    _____

    _____

4. I should never have played poker with Uncle Hal.
    himself / a full house / he / (deal) / and then four aces / first

    _____

_____

_____

5. Hank knew if he wanted to be done on time for class, he'd have to hurry.
(begin) / to type / he / his psychology paper / before class / only two hours

_____

_____

_____

6. The group's lead singer was extremely talented.
while playing keyboards / he / songs he himself wrote / (sing)

_____

_____

_____

7. Sadie hoped she could find her small silver rosebud earrings.
accidentally / (throw) / them / into the garbage / had / she

_____

_____

_____

8. I applied to the bank for a seven-thousand-dollar car loan.
the bank / me / ten thousand dollars / (lend) / instead / generously

_____

_____

_____

_____

Exercise 4-20   Using Irregular Verbs (continued)

9. The oil and vinegar in the salad dressing bottle had separated.
    however / they / after Todd / the bottle / (shake) / were well mixed

    _____

    _____

    _____

10. The shocked high school senior listened attentively to her guidance
    counselor.
    (have) / she / that college / had / so much / (cost) / no idea

    _____

    _____

    _____

11. Max's thighs and calves are really firm.
    six miles a day / he / for the last / has / (run) / five years

    _____

    _____

    _____

Exercise 4-21   Using Irregular Verbs

INSTRUCTIONS: Read the sentence carefully in the item below to discover whether the action is taking place in the present or in the past. Then use the supplied subject and verb in parentheses to write another sentence that might follow it in a composition or story. Be sure to use the correct form of the verb. Find the verb in the list provided or in a dictionary if you are not sure what form is called for. The first one is done for you.

1.   The baby smeared a piece of chocolate birthday cake all over his

   face. Meanwhile, his parents (sing) _____

   Meanwhile, his parents sang "Happy Birthday"

   to their son on his first birthday.

2.   Jennifer noticed her guests' glasses were empty. She (begin) _____

   _____

   _____

3.   Professor Atkins informed Thelma that her history term paper was

   ten pages too short. Thelma had not (write) _____

   _____

   _____

4.   Rick's sweatshirt smells funny. I think he (wear) _____

   _____

   _____

5.   Lorne is just now turning in homework that was due three weeks
   ago. He has certainly (take) _____

   _____

   _____

6. A warrant was issued for the arrest of Mr. Edwards, the bank teller. He had (steal) _____

_____

_____

7. My brother borrowed money from his fiancé to buy an engagement ring. He then (spend) _____

_____

_____

8. When he was younger, Jed could party from six in the evening to the early hours of the morning. Now, though, he (sleep) _____

_____

_____

9. The basketball team took a three-hour bus trip to Atlantic City. Unfortunately, they (sing) _____

_____

_____

10. Jim washed his cotton shorts in extremely hot water. They (shrink)

_____

_____

11. Part of the baby's ear medicine had settled at the bottom of the container. Father (shake) _____

_____

_____

Exercise 4-22 Using Irregular Verbs

INSTRUCTIONS: Read the sentence carefully in each item below to discover whether the action is taking place in the present or the past. Then use the supplied subject and verb in parentheses to write another sentence that might follow it in a composition or story. Be sure to use the correct form of the verb. Find the verb in the list provided or in a dictionary if you are not sure what form is called for. The first one is done for you.

1. Martin hadn't had any contact with his twin brother Michael for

    fifteen years. Nevertheless, Martin (send) _____

    Nevertheless, Martin sent Michael a Christmas

    card every year.

2. My neighbor Max jogged only one mile this morning. For the past

    five years he has (run) _____

    _____

    _____

3. My uncle always thought himself a very wise man. Once he

    proclaimed that, although the sun had usually (rise) _____

    _____

    _____

4. At two o'clock this morning, my sister pounded on our front door.

    Finally, after she had (ring) _____

    _____

    _____

5. The garage mechanic had suffered from a cold for two weeks. As

   he (blow) _____

   _____

6. I have always supplied refreshments at our family's Super Bowl

   party. This past January, however, my brother-in-law (bring) _____

   _____

7. Bud was elected Mayor of Centerville, having won sixty-five
   percent of the vote. Obviously he had (build) _____

   _____

8. Mrs. Bradbury had saved three hundred coupons for Feline

   catfood. She (buy) _____

   _____

9. Lee muttered unintelligibly while his teacher lectured him for being

   late. He (feel) _____

   _____

10. Lou usually brings a peanut butter sandwich to work for lunch.

    Yesterday, however, he (buy) _____

    _____

Exercise 4-23   Using Irregular Verbs

INSTRUCTIONS: Read the sentence carefully in each item below to discover whether the action is taking place in the present or the past. Then use the supplied subject and verb in parentheses to write another sentence that might precede it in a composition or story. Be sure to use the correct form of the verb. Find the verb in the list provided or in a dictionary if you're not sure what form is called for. The first one is done for you.

1. Edna (feed) <u>fed her five cats two cans of cat food</u>

    <u>each as soon as she got home.</u>

    They hadn't had a thing to eat in days.

2. I (write) _____

    _____

    _____

    Unfortunately, my dog ate it.

3. Martha (see) _____

    _____

    _____

    She thought, however, that she wouldn't mention it to her fiancé

4. Sam (drink) _____

    _____

    _____

    Nevertheless, he didn't even "place" in his first body building championship.

5. I have (go) _____

    _____

I can't imagine doing that one more time.

6. Willis (bring) _____

_____

_____

He was the most popular person at Miranda's party.

7. The medical student (become) _____

_____

_____

He wondered if he should continue to study to be a doctor.

8. Melinda had (break) _____

_____

_____

She couldn't possibly compete in Saturday's track meet.

9. While my ex-husband (ring) _____

_____

_____

I had no idea what he was after this time.

10. Silas has (drive) _____

_____

_____

It's no wonder he can hardly keep his eyes opened.

Exercise 4-24 Using Irregular Verbs

INSTRUCTIONS: In the paragraphs below, write in the correct form of the verb in the space provided. Find the verb in the list provided or in a dictionary if you are not sure what form is called for. The first two are completed for you.

1.   Marcia considered which of her two primary boyfriends she should marry, Tommy or Brian. Tommy the teacher, she recalled, (can) (1) could recite rules of grammar whenever you (give) (2) gave him the opportunity. Brian the professional gambler (go)

(3) _____ to Atlantic City at least once a week, ever since

the gambling casinos had (begin) (4) _____ to do business. Marcia loved both grammar and gambling, so she (think)

(5) _____ she (will) (6) _____ consider the matter further.
        Each (come) (7) _____ with his own advantages and

disadvantages. Tommy, for example (have) (8) _____ a severe sinus condition so that every time they (draw)

(9) _____ close to kiss, he (blow) (10) _____ his nose instead. Apologizing, he always explained that at such a moment he needed to blow his nose more than he needed to kiss.

He (speak) (11) _____ movingly of how wonderful it was

that he (feel) (12) ___ comfortable enough with his "girl" so that he (can)

(13) _____ either kiss her or blow his nose. "Such," he often

glowed, (be) (14) "_____ intimacies that some couples never

(know) (15) _____."
2.   Brian, certainly, (be) (1) _____ a whole other kettle of

fish. Brian (bring) (2) _____ excitement into Marcia's life,

but with Brian, she had also (buy) (3) _____ herself a lot of trouble. In fact, when she first (meet) (4) _____ his former

"business associate," Lenny, he (tell) (5) _____ Marcia that

Brian (can) (6) "_____ steal the eyes right out of your head
and tell you that you looked better without them." Marcia, of

course, (do) (7) _____ not believe a word Lenny (speak)

(8) _____, but she also didn't know whether she (shall)

(9) _____ trust Brian. She (catch) (10) _____
herself remembering little white lies that Brian had (tell)

(11) _____ her, like the time he (say) (12) _____

he (be) (13) _____ the long lost heir of Howard Hughes. The

more she (think) (14) _____ about it, the more she (shrink)

(15) _____ from the idea of marrying Brian. Sure, she had

(grow) (16) _____ to love the big lug, but she had (build)

(17) _____ this cardboard house of her affection on a

foundation of sand. All around her she (see) (18) _____
marriages coming apart at the seams, after physical attraction had

(lost) (19) _____ its primary importance. Therefore,

common sense (lead) (20) _____ her to the idea that

Tommy's sinuses (may) (21) _____ be more dependable
than Brian's body.

3.   And when she thought about it, Tommy, the English teacher, was

not all that boring. Together they had (know) (1) _____
some wonderfully exciting moments. There was the time they had

(eat) (2) _____ pizza with anchovies and had (drink)

(3) _____ iced tea. There was the time, too, when the doorbell

Exercise 4-24 Using Irregular Verbs (continued)

(ring) (4) _____. When Marcia (go) (5) _____ to see

who was there, she (see) (6) _____ Tommy who (sing)

(7) _____ "As Time Goes By." These romantic memories

(steal) (8) _____ into her head as she (spend)

(9) _____ most of her waking and dreaming hours thinking
about whom she should marry. It was also true that Tommy had

(write) (10) _____ her the most romantic love letters; so she
decided she shouldn't be prejudiced against his unruly sinuses. Just

as she (make) (11) _____ her decision, Tommy appeared at

the door. Marcia (fly) (12) _____ to his manly chest and

(sing) (13) _____ "All of Me! Why Not Take All of Me?"

Tommy, not knowing what to think, (fight) (14) _____ her

back, but passion had (overcome) (15) _____ her. She was

not to be denied. "What's a fella to do?" (think) (16) _____

Tommy. He (burst) (17) _____ into tears of joy; his arms

(freeze) (18) _____ in a passionate embrace. He muttered
huskily, "Take me; I'm yours, but be gentle with me, Dear!"

MAKING SUBJECTS AND VERBS AGREE

As was mentioned earlier, if an action is going on in the present, and if the subject is a singular *he, she,* or *it* (one person, one place, or one thing), you must put an *-s* ending on the verb, for example:

The student with his feet up on the cafeteria chair <u>stares</u> straight ahead.

Notice the subject is a *he,* meaning that an *-s* is required on the end of the verb:

He . . . stare<u>s</u> straight ahead.

If the subject is a plural *they* and the action is taking place in the present, do *not* attach an *-s* ending. In this example,

The reporters crowded on the capitol steps <u>take</u> notes as the governor answers their questions.

"Reporters" are a *they* subject, so no *-s* ending is necessary on the verb:

They . . . <u>take</u> notes. . . .

A compound, or double, subject is usually considered a plural *they.* In this sentence "laughing and joking" are two subjects:

Laughing and joking <u>occupy</u> much of my time.

Also, the following "-one," "-thing," and "-body" words are considered singular *he, she,* or *it* subjects.

one	nobody	nothing	each
anyone	anybody	anything	either
everyone	everybody	everything	neither
someone	somebody	something	

So when one of these words is used as a subject, it is considered a singular subject, and the *-s* ending is needed on the verb, as in:

Neither of the cereals <u>tastes</u> very good.

Each of my shoes <u>has</u> a hole in the sole.

Everyone <u>has completed</u> his or her homework.

Everybody <u>dislikes</u> Sharon.

The subject must always agree with its verb in number. If the subject is singular, the verb, too, must be singular *with* the -s ending. If the subject is plural, the verb must be plural also *without* the -s ending. This rule of English is called *agreement*.

Exercise 4-25   Making Subjects and Verbs Agree

INSTRUCTIONS: Read the sentence in each item below. Then combine the scrambled words into a complete sentence that might follow the first in a composition or story. Be sure to use the correct form of the verb in parentheses. After the subject of the new sentence, put in parentheses whether the subject is a *he, she, it,* or *they.* Remember that if the subject is a *he, she,* or *it,* add an *-s* ending to the verb in the present tense. If the subject is a *they,* no *-s* ending is required in the present tense. The first one is done for you.

1. Going to college has turned out to be much more work than I expected.
    papers and quizzes / simply (amaze) me / the number of / completed for each course

    The number (it) of papers and quizzes

    completed for each course simply amazes me.

2. Louise hopes to break into show business someday.
    among her / singing and dancing / to be / recreational activities / favorite / (seem)

    _____

    _____

    _____

3. I'm no farmer, but I do know this.
    whenever / corn and lettuce / the soil / (grow) / is dark and rich

    _____

    _____

    _____

4. The oven is much too hot.
    as if / (look) / on the bottom shelf / the cookies / they're (burn)

5. I have enjoyed reading books on all kinds of subjects ever since I could read.
of all the books / (be) / however / the most fascinating / I have (read) / about pruning trees

_____

_____

6. Vladimir can tell quite a bit about Alex's mind from his bookshelf.
(show) / that Alex / science to art / the choice of books / (prefer) / on the shelf

_____

_____

7. Hank is not at all sure that being a student is good for his health.
(make) / Hank feel / studying / as if he / several hours a day / (be) / dead from the neck down

_____

_____

8. Both Darryl and Steve have given Beth an engagement ring.
that Beth / (realize) / can have / each one / her pick of guys

_____

_____

Exercise 4-25   Making Subjects and Verbs Agree (continued)

_____

9. Although spring break lasts a week, I'll have to spend most of it
    doing homework.
    homework / teachers / I / who thoughtlessly / really dislike /
    (assign) / during vacation

    _____

    _____

    _____

10. Sibyl, my best friend, always looks so slim.
    to burn / her dancing and skating / activities that / many calories /
    (be) / (make) / it possible for her

    _____

    _____

    _____

11. The judges were very confused about whom to choose for
    homecoming queen.
    what you / neither / (be) / of the candidates / would call /
    intelligent or beautiful

    _____

    _____

    _____

Exercise 4-26   Making Subjects and Verbs Agree

INSTRUCTIONS: Read the sentence in each item below. Then combine the scrambled words into a complete sentence that might follow the first in a composition or story. Be sure to use the correct form of the verb in parentheses. After the subject of the new sentence, put in parentheses whether the subject is a *he, she, it,* or *they*. Remember that if the subject is a *he, she,* or *it*, add an -*s* ending to the verb in the present tense. If the subject is a *they*, no -*s* ending is required in the present tense. The first one is done for you.

1. Jeanette plans to spend the next fifteen years of her life learning to be a brain surgeon.
   her / soon / of her boyfriends / none / to be marrying / (expect)

   <u>None (he) of her boyfriends expects to be</u>

   <u>marrying her soon.</u>

2. Jerry, the shortstop, gets out of the locker room as quickly as possible.
   (use) / he / of the baseball team / (claim) / that the members / filthy language

   _____

   _____

3. The math student has solved most of the problems he was assigned for homework.
   can't / there / still / (be) / two equations / he / figure out

   _____

   _____

4. Mr. Smith is snapping a picture of his four-year-old daughter.
   him / playing / Emily / (do) / among the daffodils / not seem to notice

   _____

   _____

5. For months I wear long underwear, flannel shirts, and woolen sweaters.
   not keep me warm / /(do) / cups of / during the winter / hot chocolate / and photographs of Hawaii

   _____

   _____

6. No one ever remembers to feed the dogs.
   under the kitchen table / Ranger and Nicky / begging for scraps / always (be) / during supper

   _____

   _____

7. The hostess anxiously awaits her guests.
   ready / to be / everything / (seem)

   _____

   _____

8. It is certainly a good evening for sipping tea and listening to music.
   fog / the house / like a blanket / (cover) / and drizzle

   _____

   _____

9. Mattie left half of her Valentine candy uneaten.
   She explained / "I hate" / "of the chocolates that" / "caramel" / "the centers" / "(contain)"

   _____

   _____

10. Erica loves to see her Father raking leaves on a fall afternoon.
    (be) great / to play in / of leaves and twigs / the pile / fun

    _____

    _____

Exercise 4-27 Making Subjects and Verbs Agree

INSTRUCTIONS: Read the sentence in each item below and write another sentence that might follow it in a story or composition. Identify the subject of the new sentence by placing a *he, she, it,* or *they* in parentheses in front of the verb. Be sure to add an *-s* to the verb if necessary. Finally, complete the sentence so that it is detailed and logically related to the given sentence. The first one is done for you.

1. Listening to music is a much more pleasurable activity than watching television. Sore eyes and aching head often (prompt)

   (they) prompt me to desert the television set

   in order to "join" my stereo.

2. My father never takes care of his cars the way he should. The tires on his truck (look) _____

   _____

   _____

3. My husband and I crouched behind our livingroom couch. Staring in our livingroom window (be) _____

   _____

   _____

4. Ida seems to be very quick-tempered. However, anybody who (know) _____ her (realize) _____

   _____

   _____

5. I admire my sister very much. Always thinking of others first or putting herself second (show)

   _____

   _____

6. Right now our kitchen is not a pleasant place to be.
The little cabbages boiling in the iron pot (smell) _____

_____

_____

7. Everybody has favorite holidays.
Memorial Day and the last few days of school (remind) _____

_____

_____

8. Going to school is often a confusing experience.
Everything my teachers say (contradict) _____

_____

_____

9. Tim and Tony have been watching television for several hours.
Cookie crumbs and popcorn (cover) _____

_____

_____

10. A very punctual person herself, Ms. Johnson the history teacher
always starts her class exactly on time.
Ms. Johnson, when interrupted by late-comers, (ask) _____

_____

_____

11. "Don't you just love the expensive dress I'm wearing?" Lilah
inquired of her friends.
"Nobody in the world, or living on the other planets in our solar
system, (care) _____

_____

_____," they replied.

Exercise 4-28 Making Subjects and Verbs Agree

INSTRUCTIONS: Read the sentence in each item below and write
another sentence that might come before it in a composition or story.
Identify the subject of the new sentence by placing a *he, she, it,* or *they* in
parentheses in front of the verb. Be sure to add an *-s* ending to the verb
if necessary. Finally complete the sentence so that it is detailed and
logically related to the given sentence. The first one is done for you.

1. Practicing writing essays (consist of) <u>(it) consists of lots</u>

    <u>of thinking, writing, more thinking, and</u>

    <u>revising.</u>

    Up till now I have misunderstood how you go about writing a
    thoughtful essay.

2. None of my brother's girlfriends (know) _____

    _____

    _____

    I'm certainly not going to tell them.

3. The elastic band on my gym shorts (have) _____

    _____

    _____

    I'd better wear another pair of shorts underneath them.

4. Gert is the type of person who (get) _____

    _____

    _____

    But she has really enjoyed her first semester at college.

5. The difficulties of sewing (have) _____

_____

_____

He finds it difficult to thread the needle of the sewing machine.

6. Any of my classmates who (say) _____ that _____

_____

_____

None of us have been working as hard as we should be.

7. The information I get on the evening news always (involve) _____

_____

_____

I guess I shouldn't watch the news while I'm eating dinner.

8. "Your sister, her friends, their boyfriends, and the dog (treat) _____

_____

_____

I feel as if I'm running a dormitory!" complained Mother.

9. Our minister, in tears, (congratulate) _____

_____

_____

He is pleased that his Sunday school students have listened to him so carefully.

10. The subjects you study in school that (stick) _____

with you (be) _____

Exercise 4-28   Making Subjects and Verbs Agree (continued)

_____

_____

A student isn't usually the best judge of what he or she needs to learn.

11. Doing fifty push-ups and a hundred sit-ups every morning (make)

_____

_____

He plans to live until he's a hundred.

Exercise 4-29 Making Subjects and Verbs Agree

INSTRUCTIONS: Read each paragraph below through completely, and then write in the correct form of the verb. Finally, complete the sentences so that they make points that fit in logically with the other sentences in the paragraph. The first one is done for you.

1.   Although it's the wrong time of the month for one to appear, the people I see at the shopping mall this evening make me think there may be a full moon out. One of the shoppers in front of me (look) (1) <u>looks as if he has no idea how oddly he is</u> <u>dressed.</u> Wearing his T-shirt backwards and his shoelaces

untied (make) (2) _____ .

Then there (be) (3) _____

the shoppers patiently waiting to (4) _____

_____ . They appear to be quite strange too. The guy wearing the fur gloves, for example, (keep)

(5) _____ .
And then behind him two teenage boys, arguing over which one of them should eat their last chocolate chip cookie, (push)

(6) _____ .

On a bench a few feet away, playing dominoes, (sit) (7) _____

_____ the boys' mother who (signal)

(8) _____ . From time to time some band or

other, too far away to be seen, (play) (9) _____ .

Tears, slowly at first but then more quickly, (stream) (10) _____

_____ . Then, miraculously, the guy in the T-shirt, the man wearing the fur gloves, the bickering teenage boys, and their

mother (grab) (11) _____.
I'd better get to Sears, so I can buy my purple bowling shoes and
get away from all these very strange people.

2.   There are only five minutes left, and this championship basketball
game has really heated up. The Center City players and their coach

(act) (1) _____

_____. When the game started, no
one gave them a chance of winning, but now each player, his

sneakers pounding the boards, (handle) (2) _____

_____. Even the members of the

team who (remain) (3) _____

on the bench (participate) (4) _____

_____. Meanwhile, adding to

the excitement (be) (5) _____

_____ hundreds of fans who (study) (6) _____

_____

carefully every move the players (make) (7) _____

_____. Three minutes to
go; the score is 76-76, when suddenly one of the assistant coaches,

Mr. Arnold, (decide) (8) _____

_____. Nobody in

the gym (believe) (9) _____

that he (have) (10) _____

just (offer) (11) _____.
The official standing near Mr. Arnold (try) (12) _____

Exercise 4-29   Making Subjects and Verbs Agree (continued)

_____, but Mr. Arnold, knocking

over a few chairs (persist) (13) _____

_____ in _____

_____. Finally the official wearing the

bifocals (call) (14) _____ a

technical foul and (threaten) (15) _____ to

(force) (16) _____. "It took them
long enough," thinks Mr. Arnold to himself. "Now I'll have a chance
to collect my bet on the other team."

3.   I can't help but write in my journal that this is one of the most
magnificent afternoons I have ever witnessed. I can't believe I'm
here on Cape Cod on this lovely June day, quietly observing the

beauty of nature. First, the colors of the ocean (change) (1) _____

_____. The very slight ripples that the gentle

breeze (create) (2) _____

on the ocean surface (add) (3) _____

_____. The sun is just warm enough
to make me feel comfortable and secure, while gusts of wind (cool)

(4) _____.

Each sound, whether from the ocean or seagulls, (tell) (5) _____

_____. There (be) (6) _____

blessings in these sights and sounds which (cause) (7) _____

_____. The sky, its colors and clouds,

(match) (8) _____.

The pale blue sky, in places near the ocean, (reflect) (9) _____

_____. The cumulus

clouds that sometimes (seem) (10) _____

_____ to take up the whole sky as

they float by (make) (11) _____

me think of (12) _____

_____. A beautiful scene like this,

which (include) (13) _____

_____, (teach) (14) _____

_____ me that (15) _____

_____. Every one of us

(have) (16) _____ to

wait for (17) _____;
when they come, they're certainly rewarding.

USING PRONOUNS

Pronouns are words that take the place of nouns so that we don't have to keep repeating the nouns. Some pronoun forms can be a substitute for nouns that are the subjects of sentences. For example, all these pronouns can be subjects:

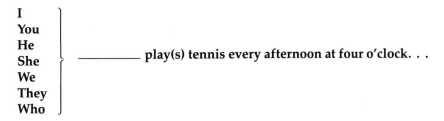

I
You
He
She
We
They
Who

} ———————— play(s) tennis every afternoon at four o'clock. . .

Other pronoun forms can receive the actions of verbs as in:

Our teacher appreciates ———————
{
me
you
him
her . . .
us
them
whom
}

These pronouns are called the *direct object* of the verb because they receive the action of the verb.

These same direct-object forms are used after prepositions:

The mailman handed the new phone book to ———————————
{
me
you
him
her . . .
us
them
whom
}

In this case the pronouns are called the *object of the preposition* "to."

Sometimes you will use one of these pronouns with another pronoun or noun. You still need to choose a pronoun from the subject-group to be a subject and a pronoun from the object-group to receive the action of a verb or to follow a preposition. Test out whether you've chosen the right form by reading the sentence aloud, reading only one pronoun-part at a time:

As for (Martha and) <u>me</u>, (she and) <u>I</u> wouldn't be caught dead in that place.

Les confronted (Joanne and) <u>him</u> with the bad news.

(Lawrence and) <u>she</u> knows only four languages, not five.

One other set of pronouns act as adjectives, answering the questions "Which kind of _____?" or "What _____ do you mean?" They answer these questions by telling *whose* person, place, or thing is being referred to. For example:

Whose glasses are lying there on the skating rink?

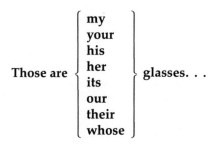

Those are { my your his her its our their whose } glasses. . .

The following pronouns are considered to be *he, she,* or *it* subjects in written English, so they must be used with "his," "him," "her," or "its":

everyone	everybody	one
anyone	anybody	either
someone	nobody	neither
each	no one	

Has anyone forgotten his or her umbrella?

Neither of the nurses opened her or his eyes while she or he drew her or his patient's blood.

There's one more pronoun form to watch out for: the *reflexive* pronoun. This is the form that has "self" or "selves" attached to it:

myself	ourselves
yourself	yourselves
himself, herself, itself	themselves

These forms should be used only to "reflect back" on the subject:

I like <u>myself</u> better and better everyday.

The doctors prepared <u>themselves</u> for surgery.

Finally, avoid using "hisself" or "theirself" when you write.

Exercise 4-30   Using Pronouns

INSTRUCTIONS: For each item below, read the given sentence carefully, and then combine the scrambled words following it into a sentence. Use whichever pronoun is called for. The first one is done for you.

1. Nelson and Eddie practiced their duet for the upcoming church minstrel show.
    together / quite sure / that (pronoun) voices / (pronoun) weren't / would sound good

    <u>They weren't quite sure that their voices</u>

    <u>would sound good together.</u>

2. Writing on long, yellow paper makes everything I write look official.
    even / better / looks / (pronoun) sloppy / on (pronoun) / handwriting

    _____

    _____

3. After his company left, Father demanded to know why we children had behaved so badly.
    "was boring" / "and" / "(pronoun) had" / "(pronoun) company" / "nothing else to do," / (pronoun) explained

    _____

    _____

4. Constance piled your blue-willow dishes in the cupboard very gingerly.
    just as careful / (pronoun) was / (pronoun) replaced / when / (pronoun) crystal goblets

    _____

    _____

5. The ballroom dancers swayed as one, as if directed by an invisible choreographer.
   into one another / suddenly as if (pronoun) / (pronoun) bumped / directed (pronoun) no more

   _____

   _____

6. The twins, Tess and Trixie, fed their breakfast bananas to their dog Rex.
   (pronoun) / much more / (pronoun) appreciated / than (pronoun) did

   _____

   _____

7. Each of the husbands serenaded his wife on the occasion of their twenty-fifth wedding anniversary.
   One of (pronoun) / on (pronoun) own guitar / accompanied (pronoun)

   _____

   _____

8. Application in hand, Cody looked around the room at all the office workers sitting behind well-ordered desks.
   (pronoun) should hand (pronoun) / (pronoun) wasn't sure / to (pronoun)

   _____

   _____

9. Four-year-old Harry helped three-year-old Zelda on with her coat; then Zelda tied Harry's shoes.
   "(pronoun) believe" / commented Zelda / "people should" / "help one another"

   _____

   _____

Exercise 4-30   Using Pronouns (continued)

10. When her co-star handed her the wrong prop, the actress forgot
    her lines.
    after calming (pronoun) down / and began to speak / (pronoun)
    remembered (pronoun)

    _____

    _____

11. Our daughter Maria expects her father and me to buy her a Porsche
    and pay for her tuition at Yale.
    on (pronoun) father and (pronoun) / for everything / (pronoun) am
    afraid / that (pronoun) depends

    _____

    _____

12. "My friend Jeff has gotten engaged for the fourth time," I informed
    my wife.
    "now" / "to marry" / she inquired / "(pronoun) has he decided"

    _____

    _____

13. This morning I was shocked to discover my sister Luiz's tropical
    fish floating belly-up in the fish tank.
    buried (pronoun) / under the front porch steps / Lucy and
    (pronoun) / in tears

    _____

    _____

14. While we were taking our math test, Lester asked me to borrow a
    pencil.

slamming her book / Ms. Marlowe / asked Lester and (pronoun) /
shut / to leave the room

_____

_____

15. The starting five of the basketball team missed five shots,
    committed six fouls, and forgot their plays.
    to discuss what / gathered together / the coach and (pronoun) /
    (pronoun) should do next

_____

_____

16. Mr. Jones had not quite completed his remarks on the differences
    between Greek and Roman culture.
    out the door / (pronoun) book / so that (pronoun) / everyone
    closed / could be the first one / nevertheless

_____

_____

Exercise 4-31   Using Pronouns

INSTRUCTIONS: For each item below, read the given sentence carefully. Then write out the correct pronoun and complete the following sentence so that it fits in with the meaning of the first sentence. The first one is done for you.

1.   Lea's new father-in-law shook her hand limply while her new mother-in-law simply pecked her on the cheek.
     Lea concluded that (pronoun) new in-laws

     Lea concluded that her new in-laws weren't

     thrilled to have her as their new daughter-

     in-law.

2.   I didn't like the car my parents bought, and neither did my brothers.
     (Pronoun) agreed that (pronoun) parents probably

     _____

     _____

3.   Jane and Artie expressed their sympathies to Mrs. Norwick, whose husband had just died.
     Sadly (pronoun) recalled how (pronoun) friend, Mr. Norwick had

     _____

     _____

4.   "Which one of the cheerleaders do you find the most attractive?" Pete asked Charlie.
     Charlie replied, "(pronoun) can't take (pronoun) eyes off the one (pronoun) keeps

     _____

     _____

5. The vice principal has interrogated every single student who was in the gym today.
   Still, nobody seems to know (pronoun) sneaker is

   _____

   _____

6. My cat, which disappeared about a week ago, returned home hungry and exhausted.
   After it licked (pronoun) paws, (pronoun)

   _____

   _____

7. Bernie, Paul, and I have been friends for years, but the other day Paul and I saw another side of Bernie.
   (Pronoun) became very angry with Paul and (pronoun) when (pronoun) realized that (pronoun)

   _____

   _____

8. Lemar and his sister shopped at the mall for several hours last Saturday.
   Both Lemar and (pronoun) have been invited to

   _____

   _____

9. Alicia Smithe, the president of Merchant's Bank, speaks four languages fluently.
   No one has ever said about (pronoun) that (pronoun)

   _____

   _____

10. When he sat down, three-hundred-pound Uncle Charley broke the legs off of grandmother's rocker.

Exercise 4-31   Using Pronouns (continued)

After (pronoun) gathered (pronoun) pieces together, (pronoun)

_____

_____

11. Kim and Tim adjusted the timing on the engine of Kim's Camaro.
    In the past (pronoun) and (pronoun) had often

_____

_____

12. General Custer and the Indians discussed who should surrender in
    order to end the long battle.
    In the opinion of both (pronoun) and (pronoun), dying on the
    plains of South Dakota

_____

_____

13. Rhonda has always disagreed with her sorority sisters about the
    type of people who should be invited to join their sorority.
    (Pronoun), unlike (pronoun), looks for people (pronoun)

_____

_____

14. The plumber and his two apprentices replaced the burst pipe in
    about an hour.
    Working together as a team, (pronoun) and (pronoun) quickly

_____

_____

15. My best friend Ernest and I have done everything together since grade school.
When we have a test, for example, (pronoun) and (pronoun) first

_____

_____

16. Studying and learning, whether in high school or college, take real dedication and work.
Anyone (pronoun) tries to fake it fools (pronoun) when (pronoun)

_____

_____

Exercise 4-32   Using Pronouns

INSTRUCTIONS: Read the paragraphs below very carefully. Then write in the pronoun called for. The first one is done for you.

1. Tommie and his friends Warren and Ed had a long history of not doing well in school. Now that they had somehow gotten (pronoun)

(1) __themselves__ into college, (pronoun) (2) _____

wondered whether (pronoun) (3) _____ should try to stay

there. Tommie and (pronoun) (4) _____ seemed to act the

same way in college as (pronoun) (5) _____ had in high

school, but suddenly Tommie wondered if (pronoun) (6) _____

wanted the same things as (pronoun) (7) _____ did.

   Tommie first reconsidered (pronoun) (8) _____

relationship with Warren and Ed after (pronoun) (9) _____

overheard some classmates talking about (pronoun)(10) _____

before class. One student mentioned to another that (pronoun)

(11) _____ was tired of Warren's and Ed's coming to class
late, interrupting the professor as she tried to explain a very
complicated idea in a very short period of time. "As if that isn't bad

enough," (pronoun) (12) _____ complained, "then

(pronoun) (13) _____ usually ask if the class has

accomplished anything important since (pronoun) (14) _____

were last in class! (Pronoun) (15) _____ can imagine how

they acted when (pronoun) (16) _____ were in high school!

(Pronoun) (17) _____ are eighteen-year-old high school graduates!"

Tommie suddenly saw (pronoun) (18) _____ and his friends in a wholly different light. (Pronoun) (19) _____ fellow students saw (pronoun) (20) _____ friends as having mature bodies but immature minds. Tommie wondered if (pronoun) (21) _____ might not have the same attitude toward (pronoun) (22) _____ . (Pronoun) (23) _____ thought that (pronoun) (24) _____ should reconsider why (pronoun) (25) _____ was in college and to what extent (pronoun) (26) _____ was taking responsibility for (pronoun) (27) _____ own future. (Pronoun) (28) _____ was ashamed of (pronoun) (29) _____ . Could Tommie alert (pronoun) (30) _____ friends to (pronoun) (31) _____ own immaturity just as (pronoun) (32) _____ had come to realize (pronoun) (33) _____ own?

2.   Even though I know it's a natural part of being alive, I've never gotten used to being sick or, for that matter, to my family's being sick. Even when (pronoun) (1) _____ was a kid, (pronoun) (2) _____ remember how (pronoun) (3) _____ mother would try to keep (pronoun) (4) _____ in bed when (pronoun) (5) _____ was sick. Sometimes, when both (pronoun) (6) _____ sister and (pronoun) (7) _____ were sick, (pronoun) (8) _____ would try to keep both of

Exercise 4-32   Using Pronouns (continued)

(pronoun) (9) _____ in bed. Often mother made (pronoun)

(10) _____ sick carting untasted meals upstairs and down, making mild threats as to what would happen if (pronoun)

(11) _____ didn't eat.
    As I grew older and became as aware of others' problems as

(pronoun) (12) _____ was of (pronoun) (13) _____

own, (pronoun) (14) _____ parents' or grandparents'

getting sick reminded (pronoun) (15) _____ of all (pronoun)

(16) _____ had done for (pronoun) (17) _____

when (pronoun) (18) _____ had been ill. (Pronoun)

(19) _____ being sick also reminded me that (pronoun)

(20) _____ and (pronoun) (21) _____ wouldn't always be together.
    My grandmother has been very ill now for about a year, and

during that time, (pronoun) (22) _____ has taught me a lot about sickness being unavoidable in life. And even though

(pronoun) (23) _____ is very sick, (pronoun) (24) _____

claims that being sick reminds all of (pronoun) (25) _____

that (pronoun) (26) _____ are very fortunate to have

whatever health (pronoun) (27) _____ do have. (Pronoun)

(28) _____ believes that everyone has (pronoun)

(29) _____ or (pronoun) (30) _____ own imperfections and that to be alive means to perfect yourself as much

as possible, under whatever conditions (pronoun) (31) _____

find (pronoun) (32) _____ . (Pronoun) (33) _____
says that sickness can be a challenge, even a vocation. (Pronoun)

(34) _____ point of view amazes (pronoun) (35) _____ .

(Pronoun) (36) _____ am not so afraid of sickness as

(pronoun) (37) _____ used to be.

Exercise 4-33   Making Subjects, Verbs, and Pronouns Agree

INSTRUCTIONS: Read through the following composition completely and carefully. Then rewrite it completely, changing the plural "workers" to the singular "worker." You will have to rewrite verbs and pronouns in order to make them agree with your new singular subject, "a worker." The first paragraph is done for you.

These days workers' jobs have become more and more complicated. In fact, workers don't seem to work in the same way workers of twenty years ago did.

They don't run so much heavy machinery anymore, and those who work on assembly lines are being replaced by robots—machines that are run by other machines. Machines known as computers are the brains that run the machines that make and turn the nuts and bolts of still other machines.

The new workers are the people who program the computers and the people who maintain the computers and the machines they operate. Workers today have to understand what the computer needs to know in order to do its work and how to make the computer do the job it and they have "in mind." Workers today have to work more with their brains than with their hands. They are no longer "manu-facturers"; they are "techno-facturers."

Workers in today's economy, in other words, have to become more skilled at using their minds than their bodies.

These days a worker's job has become more and more

complicated. In fact, a worker doesn't seem to

work in the same way a worker of twenty years

ago did.

Exercise 4-34   Making Subjects, Verbs, and Pronouns Agree

INSTRUCTIONS: Read through the following composition completely and carefully. Then rewrite it completely, changing the singular "a student" to the plural "students." You will have to change verbs and pronouns in order to agree with your new plural subject "students." The first paragraph is done for you.

A true student really does two things when she studies: she analyzes and she synthesizes.

When she is confronted with something she doesn't know or understand, she learns to analyze it or take it apart. She does this until she understands the parts that make up the thing she wasn't able to understand before. The "thing" may be a problem in engineering class or a novel like *War and Peace* in literature class. Her work is still the same, however: and that is, with the teacher's guidance, to pull the thing apart to see how it works.

The other kind of "unknown" a student is faced with is a collection of items that don't seem to have any connection to one another. She doesn't see what the items have in common, if anything. When finally she does see how the items are really parts of a whole, she has "synthesized" them into something known or understandable. She may be presented with parts that may be put together to make an electric motor; or, she may be given the symptoms of a sick person that can be related in such a way as to suggest a diagnosis of the person's sickness.

Whichever activity of the mind she is pursuing, analysis or synthesis, she can be sure of this: truly educating herself is a matter of doing one or the other.

_____

True students really do two things when they

study: they analyze and they synthesize.

_____

_____

_____

_____

_____

USING COMMAS

Often beginning writers use too many commas. It's as if they sense that their word order or sentence structure is confused, so, to compensate, they add a comma-stroke here and a comma-stroke there. Instead, writers should depend as much as possible on word choice and word order to make their meaning clear, not so much on crutches like commas. Commas help your readers work their way through your sentences, but only if your sentences are well written and if your commas are placed according to a *few* commonly accepted rules.

Discussion in previous sections have already introduced some of the rules about using commas, and you've seen examples of using commas in many sentences throughout these pages—like the sentences you're reading now. From our discussion about combining related sentences (pages 000-00), you already know to place a comma in front of *and, but, nor, or, for, yet,* and *so* when they connect two complete thoughts. This is the first comma rule.

Another comma rule places a comma after introductory remarks. "Introductory remarks" are the words at the beginning of a sentence that set the "scene" for the sentence's subject and verb. They provide signals or details that will only make sense when you reach the sentence's main subject and verb. The introductory remarks are underlined in the following examples:

<u>In the middle of the night</u>, I thought seriously about deserting my friend Elena who was sleeping on a cot on the other side of the cabin.

<u>Since I was shaking with fear and turning blue with the cold</u>, I thought about deserting my friend Elena who was sleeping on a cot on the other side of the cabin.

Placing a comma after introductory details allows readers to grasp the meaning before they are asked to relate it to the nucleus of the sentence, its subject and verb. These are most likely details you wish to emphasize:

When did you think seriously about deserting your friend?
In the middle of the night.

Under what circumstances did you consider deserting your friend?
I was shaking with fear and turning blue with the cold.

By observing this comma rule, you've set the scene of the sentence before you've brought the actor, the subject, center stage to perform the action of the verb.

In summary these and other commonly accepted comma rules tell us to use commas only to

1. Separate two complete thoughts connected by *and, but, nor, or, for, yet,* or *so.*

    I didn't pay the monthly installment on my new television set, <u>so</u> the finance company took it away.

2. Separate introductory words from the subject and verb of the sentence.

    <u>Until all the students have arrived for class</u>, Mr. Jenkins won't hand out the final exam.

3. Separate items in a series.

    Nick wore <u>a navy blue blazer</u>, <u>gray flannel pants</u>, and <u>white shoes</u> to the park.

4. Separate the quoted from the unquoted part of the sentence.

    "If I stick one toe into that bath water<u>,</u>" whined Abe to his father<u>,</u>" my heart will stop!"

5. Separate interruptions, or extra information, in a sentence from the main part of the sentence (these commas act somewhat like parentheses).

    My father<u>, a respectful man if there ever was one,</u> never allowed us children to refer to our mother as "she" or "her."

Exercise 4-35   Using Commas

INSTRUCTIONS: Read the sentence in each item below. Then combine the scrambled words into another sentence. Place commas where needed. The first one is done for you.

1. Late for school this morning, Tina forgot three books she needed for class.
    she / without her algebra book / left home / her English composition text / and her dictionary

    <u>She left home without her algebra book, her</u>

    <u>English composition text, and her dictionary.</u>

2. Somebody knocked on my front door just as I was climbing upstairs to bed.
    "Who is it!" / came back / I / muttering and cursing / downstairs / and shouted

    _____

    _____

    _____

3. Mervin's pet parakeet escaped from its cage.
    flew out / fresh paper / while Mervin put / it suddenly / on the floor of the cage

    _____

    _____

    _____

4. Jake whistled "Red River Valley" as he waited for the school bus.
    much / the song / he / but it was / didn't like / he knew / the only one

    _____

_____

_____

5. Frances leaned over to kiss her boyfriend just before she boarded
    the ferris wheel.
    chattered / her knees / her teeth / and her stomach / knocked /
    gurgled / as she waited for the ride to start

_____

_____

_____

6. He rolled up the bottoms of his jeans before he dangled his feet in
    the cold water.
    than usual / his feet / looked / which were always / no colder /
    bluish

_____

_____

_____

7. The hunter squatted on the ground to see if he could find any more
    deer tracks.
    "they seemed" / "right here" / he related / "to have stopped" / to
    his friend

_____

_____

_____

8. Charlene measured the material for the drapes she intended to
    make.
    a fortune / would cost / so she decided / so much material / a
    cheaper kind / to buy

_____

Exercise 4-35 Using Commas (continued)

_____

_____

9. All was peaceful and cozy in my bedroom last night.
    on the bed / lay sleeping / and / my cat / underneath / slept /
    my dog

_____

_____

_____

10. The gymnast stretched out her body as she prepared to compete.
    too hard / a hamstring / she / working her legs / pulled

_____

_____

_____

11. Mrs. Jimenez blindfolded Debbie and then turned her around three
    times.
    "take this" / "I'll walk" / "trip over a chair" / "if you don't" /
    "blindfold off" / "into a wall" / she complained / "or step on the
    cat's tail"

_____

_____

_____

12. The mother coaxed her daughter on stage.
    to herself / she thought / "start singing" / "to keep her off my
    back" / "I'd better"

_____

13. Cyril concluded he'd better get himself to the emergency room.
    nor bandaged it / badly infected / since he had / his cut had
    become / neither cleaned

14. Jeremiah quickly delivered his valedictory address and then
    disappeared from the stage.
    and modest man / takes credit / a quiet / for anything / he never

15. After a hard day's work, Harold was delighted to have finally
    gotten home.
    to pick up the laundry / he realized / the car / just as he / in the
    driveway / parked / that he had forgotten

Exercise 4-36 Using Commas

INSTRUCTIONS: Read the sentence in each item below. Then, following the directions given, write a follow-up sentence and place commas where needed. The first one is done for you.

1. Bertha was surprised to see what Kathleen was serving for Sunday brunch. (Write a sentence naming three "surprising" dishes that turned up at Kathleen's Sunday brunch.)

    She had never been offered dry champagne,

    strawberries, and Russian caviar for brunch

    before.

2. The cat sniffed around every corner in the kitchen. (Write a second sentence beginning with "Suddenly arching its back and letting out a screech.")

    _____

    _____

    _____

3. My hair stylist snapped at me for being late for my appointment. (Begin the next sentence with the hair stylist's name, followed by the phrase "usually a very mild-mannered person," then complete the sentence.)

    _____

    _____

    _____

4. I tried to explain to the police officer that I didn't deserve the ticket he was writing out. (Quote exactly your words to the police officer; in the middle of the quote where appropriate, use the phrase "I sobbed.")

    _____

5. My mornings are entirely different when I don't have to get up for school. (Write a second sentence relating two ways you spend your mornings when you don't have to get up for school. Start the sentence with "First I"; then introduce the second part of your sentence with "and then I.")

_____

_____

_____

6. The musicians at Margo's wedding played all kinds of music. (Write a sentence naming three different kinds of music they played; right next to one of the kinds of music you name, write the phrase "which is my favorite.")

_____

_____

_____

7. The bank teller refused to cash my personal check. (Write out his exact words to you; start the sentence with the words "Not looking me straight in the eye, he mumbled.")

_____

_____

_____

8. Terry does well in some sports, not so well in others. (Write a second sentence beginning with "he scored"; complete that idea and connect it with the second half of the sentence beginning with "but he loses his.")

_____

Exercise 4-36   Using Commas (continued)

_____

_____

9. Ricardo volunteered to make Thanksgiving dinner. (Write a second
    sentence beginning with "However, having taken the turkey out of
    the refrigerator.")

    _____

    _____

    _____

10. Reenie dreamed of one day owning a Porsche. (Write a second
    sentence beginning with the reason why she couldn't make her
    dream come true. Use the word "so" to connect that with a
    statement that tells how she planned to make her dream come
    true.)

    _____

    _____

    _____

11. My girlfriend told me to "get lost," I "totaled" my Trans Am, and
    my best friend told me a dead bear could play better basketball than
    I could. (Write a second sentence beginning with the words "This is
    one of those days when I say to myself"; follow this by your name,
    and then complete the sentence.)

    _____

    _____

    _____

12. "Several elements go into making a good ball player," said the coach. (Write a second sentence naming three characteristics that make a good ball player. Start your sentence with: "A good ball player must be"; then complete the sentence with "he declared.")

_____

_____

_____

13. "You've got a very important decision to make about your future here as an employee," my boss advised me. (Write a second sentence beginning with "Either you," closing the sentence with "he insisted.")

_____

_____

_____

14. After having been lost for several hours, little Artie was found eating an ice cream cone at the Central Park Zoo. (Write a second sentence beginning with "Relieved and exasperated at the same time"; then state what Artie's mother said to him.)

_____

_____

_____

15. At her garage sale, someone happily gave Elaine fifty dollars for her worn livingroom rug. (Write a second sentence beginning with "The rug." Continue with the phrase "which looked," and then complete the sentence.)

_____

_____

_____

Exercise 4-37   Using Commas

INSTRUCTIONS: Read through each paragraph below. Insert commas where needed. The first sentence is done for you.

1.	After years of not being interested in reading, Charlie has suddenly become an avid reader. He enjoys reading all kinds of books: history books science books fiction and even mathematics books. Although it sounds silly he never realized that to understand something you hadn't understood before was fun even a sign of life. "I'm already eighteen years old and I realize now how much I've missed" he said to himself. It may be hard to believe but until recently he had never even heard of the French Revolution. Names like Cleopatra Galileo and Darwin meant nothing to him. Many words names and ideas brought no thoughts to his mind. In fact almost nothing went on in his mind except saying to himself "I'm bored! What should I do now?" Often he would say to himself "My body seems grown but my mind still seems puny." Imitating his scholarly best friend Chet he began to ask questions about politics history literature and science. Once he started discussing these things and reading about them he just couldn't stop. "Life isn't so boring as I thought" he admitted to himself. "I can actually think!"

2.	During the past few months I've become embarrassed to discover that I'm a very impatient person. What is worse I am beginning to realize that impatience is a vice that may seem minor but it really says something quite "major" about my view of others. The more I think about it the more I conclude that in most cases my impatience results from my thinking of myself first. My impatience often shows up for example when I'm driving to or from work. That's usually when I find myself behind someone driving too slow someone accelerating too slowly or someone stopping to look at a street sign. What never occurs to me is that all these people have reasons for acting this way. Although they're not trying to frustrate me I may feel so. Like me they're only trying to lead their own lives. My impatience I have suddenly realized results from worrying about my getting through my own day instead of helping others get through theirs. "If I were thinking about other people" I say to myself "I wouldn't have so much time to become impatient myself." Now when I wait for what seems to be an especially long traffic light I think to myself "I hope the other people waiting for this light aren't worrying too much about it. Anxiety and impatience never made anybody happy."

FORMING POSSESSIVES

An efficient way of showing that something "belongs" to someone or something else is to use the possessive form. Usually add an apostrophe and *s* (*'s*) to the owner. For example,

my friend's broken leg
the book's binding
my sister-in-law's car
a month's pay
John's idea
men's watches
women's shoes

If the owner already ends in *s*, simply add an apostrophe:

the Jones boys' pet iguana
her sons' toys
the Jones' home
the players' spirit

Exercise 4-38 Forming Possessives

INSTRUCTIONS: Read through each of the following compositions. Then go back and change each underlined part to its possessive form by writing the possessive form right above it. The first one is done for you.

1. Melvin decided it was time to fulfill his <u>New Year's resolution</u>.
<u>resolution of the New Year</u>.

He was going to return all the items he had borrowed from his

friends. First he investigated <u>the contents of his closet</u>. In the far

corner on his right, he spied <u>the tennis racquet that belonged to his</u>

<u>friend Dennis</u>. On top of that lay <u>the cover of the racquet</u> and <u>a can of</u>

<u>tennis balls he had borrowed from Dennis' twin sister Denise</u>. "I'm a

real mooch," he admitted to himself.

Disgusted with himself, he disconsolately threw himself on his

bed, only to recall that he was lying on the pillow he had stolen from

<u>the bed of his brother Harvey</u>. Now he was thoroughly frightened;

everything of his he touched seemed to turn into <u>something that</u>

<u>belonged to somebody else</u>.

"I'll distract myself on the basketball court," he grumbled as he put

on <u>the tee shirt that belonged to his sister</u> and <u>the shorts that</u>

<u>belonged to his other brother Richard</u>. As he dribbled the basketball,

he suddenly recalled that it was <u>one he had taken from school</u>. Now

he was getting spooked: "Does nothing I have really belong to me?"

he screamed.

Running back upstairs to his room, he ripped off all the clothes that belonged to his brother and sister and stared at himself in the mirror. At that point, he was peaceful again, because what he saw in the mirror was the body of Arnold Schwarzenegger and the face of Robert Redford. "Now, I'm back to my old self," he purred.

2.	Some years later Melvin married Marissa, and, like all newlyweds, they were faced with the problem of furnishing their apartment. Melvin remembered how easily in the past he had borrowed clothes and equipment belonging to others, so he thought he'd put these skills back to work. He had gotten out of practice since he had, lately, supplied himself with worldly possessions that belonged to Marissa.

"Let's see," he said to himself, "that three-thousand-dollar sound system of Uncle Jake can't be of much use to him since he's gotten a hearing aid, so I'm sure he'd lend me that for a year or two. Furthermore, the second car belonging to my cousin Charles would be little use to Charles while he is, as they say, "paying his debt to society."

Then there was the matter of gathering dishes and glasses and pots and pans. "The fine china, antique silver, and lead crystal that my grandmother owns is hard for her to get any use out of; I could borrow that for a while—at least until I inherit it!" "Hon!" he called

Exercise 4-38 Forming Possessives (continued)

to Marissa, "this is really simple! Why do people make such a big deal of putting things together when they get married!"

Now his mind was racing with plots and plans, not to say pots and pans; he couldn't stop it, not even to sleep. In the middle of the night he'd devise ways of removing the recliner of his father to his own living room. He positively drooled when he thought of the video cassette recorder belonging to his friend Jarvis. "He gets so little use out of it," said Melvin.

Marissa, meanwhile, was not as deceived as Melvin thought. She was becoming suspicious of the ways of Melvin. "What if he decides that he wants to borrow the paycheck that belongs to his wife or the wife that belongs to the best friend of Melvin? Why didn't I see this before?" she gasped. "I'll not stay the wife of Melvin under these conditions." And so the wife of Melvin became the ex-wife of Melvin. It seemed the possessiveness of Melvin had finally caught him up.

USING CAPITAL LETTERS

Over the years people who have written English have agreed to use capital letters to signal to their readers that

1. A word is the first word in a sentence or a quoted sentence.

   My math teacher looks like Santa Claus.

   Leonard blurted out, "My math teacher looks like Santa Claus!"

2. The writer is speaking in the first person.

   I just can't fathom people who always talk about themselves.

3. The words are part of a title (except for articles and prepositions).

   My grandfather often plays "Moonlight in Vermont" on the piano.

   I'm reading a fascinating composition entitled "Words Are Your Friends."

   No one ever wished that *Gone with the Wind* was any longer.

4. A word names a particular place.

   Constance graduated from Keveny Memorial Academy on Remsen Street in Cohoes, New York.

5. A word names a day, month, or holiday.

   Was it President Roosevelt who decided that Thanksgiving should fall on the last Thursday in November?

6. A word names a trademarked product.

   On my cucumber sandwiches I prefer Hellman's to White Rose mayonnaise.

7. A word names an organization.

   I'm a real "joiner"; I belong to the Elks, the Shriners, the Masons, the Parent Teachers Association, and the Rotary Club.

8. A word names a family relation, *without* a possessive pronoun like "my" in front of it.

    <u>M</u>other and <u>F</u>ather haven't told me about my trust fund yet, so I guess I'll ask my aunt about it.

9. A word names a title used along with the person's name.

    My <u>r</u>eading <u>t</u>eacher, Professor Duncan, rubs me the wrong way.

10. A word names a language.

    I much prefer <u>P</u>ig <u>L</u>atin to any other language.

11. A word names a geographical location.

    Does everyone in the <u>M</u>idwest have blond hair and blue eyes, or is that only in the <u>W</u>est?

12. A word names an event or period in history.

    My grandchildren have no idea what it was to live through both the <u>G</u>reat <u>D</u>epression and <u>W</u>orld <u>W</u>ar II; how could they?

13. A word names a specific course.

    I tend to confuse <u>S</u>ociology 101 with <u>P</u>sychology 101 since they are both social sciences.

14. A word names a nationality or race.

    Cervantes was a <u>S</u>panish author whose book *Don Quixote* made possible the development of the modern <u>E</u>nglish novel.

Exercise 4-39   Using Capital Letters

INSTRUCTIONS: In the compositions below, the first letter of some words has been omitted. After you've read each sentence and figured out what the letter ought to be, decide whether it ought to be a capital letter or not, and then write it in. The first one is done for you.

1.　　　　Gert knew (1) _s_ he could no longer put it off. She had to study

for her college entrance (2) __xams. It was now (3) __ovember 1,

and the exam would be given on (4) __ecember 1. She wondered,

(5) "__here should I start? I know so (6) __ittle!" She wasn't

thinking about holidays like (7) __hanksgiving or

(8) __hristmas; (9) __he was only thinking of how much she didn't

know about math, (10) __conomics, history, and (11) __nglish.

　　"I've spent almost four years at Lynchberg (12) __igh

(13) __chool, and what do (14) __ have to show for it? (15) __

should have studied harder. If I heard a real-live (16) __rofessor
talk, I probably wouldn't know what he was talking about."

　　The first subject she had to review was (17) __istory; she had

taken (18) __istory 203, but she really did not know the (19) __ivil

(20) __ar from the (21) __dustrial (22) __evolution. She did know,

however, that she should have paid more attention to her

(23) __istory (24) __eacher. She picked up a book called (25) __ow

to (26) __ass *College Entrance Tests Without* (27) __nowing

(28) __nything.

Soon, though, she got bored. She daydreamed about sunning herself on the beach in (29) ___t. (30) ___auderdale, Florida. She recalled that the (31) ___oung (32) ___epublicans were sponsoring a trip there next (33) ___arch. She hoped she could put in enough hours as a cashier at (34) ___oolworth's to be able to join all the partiers in (35) ___lorida. Then she remembered she was supposed to be studying for her future. She didn't want to spend the rest of her days doing her time in Lynchberg (36) ___igh (37) ___chool, but then again, wouldn't she have to put in more time, perhaps even studying, if she went to (38) ___ollege?

Then inspiration struck: (39) ___he would apply to a (40) ___ollege in Ft. Lauderdale. (41) ___urely, a Ft. Lauderdale (42) ___chool wouldn't require her to know anything boring like Einstein's (43) ___heory of (44) ___elativity. Instead, she might have to know who was buried in (45) ___rant's (46) ___omb. Yes, Ft. Lauderdale was the place for her.

2.　　Ronald recalled all the exciting experiences he had had on his last vacation. He spent his (1) ___ummer vacation at (2) ___lantic ___ity, New Jersey, from (3) ___uly 1 to (4) ___ugust 15. He wrote in his diary: (5) "___ almost got trapped into marriage."

He had, one (6) ___fternoon, noticed a (7) ___erson drinking (8) ___ome brand of ginger ale at a beach-side hotdog stand called (9) ___ethro's. In her (10) ___eft hand, she was holding a (11) ___ook entitled (12) ___ow to Make Your Own Opportunities! Immediately Ronald said to himself, (13) "___his is the (14) ___oman I've been

Exercise 4-39   Using Capital Letters (continued)

looking for all my life! (15) __he's going to the top, and (16) __'m going with her!" He sat down beside her and looked at the menu

spelled out on the chalkboard. (17) "__ don't like (18) __reamy

brand ice cream, but I see that they also sell (19) __ld __moothie."

(20) __e still had not spoken to her directly.

Ronald thought this young (21) __ady was very beautiful, but

(22) __e wondered if their backgrounds could possibly be similar.

Was she, for example, an (23) __merican or an illegal alien? Was she,

like him, a Quaker or was she (24) __ethodist? Did she like

(25) __iller beer, or did she like Budweiser? Was she a Republican

or a (26) __emocrat?

He hoped that, like him, she had liked math better than

(27) __nglish and (28) __rench better than any other modern

language. He wanted to ask (29) __er if she would agree to live with

him in the (30) __outhwest instead of the Northeast.
However, now that he looked at her more closely, she didn't look

to be the (31) __ind of person who would help him pay for his

longed for trip through (32) __ndia and (33) __sia. In fact, she didn't

even offer to pay for his ice cream. (34) "__he's not for me," (35) __e said to himself. As he left, he spoke his first and last words to her:

"Goodbye, (36) __orgeous; we could have been so happy together."